This excellent book is a joy t
the passion and commitment t
has been so much the focus of the EMA over the last 15
years. In an age when the authority of Scripture is often
questioned and preaching scorned, the Assembly has stood
firm on the need to expound God's Word in a modern and
relevant way while upholding its full authority. From the
joyful, heart-warming exposition of Romans 8 to profound
reflections on preaching in a rapidly changing world, from
lectures on preaching heaven and hell to teaching on aspects
of biblical faith, this book wonderfully captures the feel of
the Assembly.

Revd. Dr. Paul Gardner,
Vicar of Hartford and Rural Dean

These superb addresses are the pick of the crop. They are
absolute gold dust. I recommend this book enthusiastically
and with joy.

Wallace Benn,
Bishop of Lewes

The Annual Evangelical Ministry Assembly has become a
high point of the year for many ministers throughout the United
Kingdom. Its hallmarks are: theological and practical teaching
coupled with incisive biblical exposition, all set in a context
of open and welcoming fellowship. This compilation of
carefully edited addresses is an excellent sampler of the
Assembly itself. More than that, it provides the kind of
instructive teaching and preaching which will serve to
strengthen the ministry of the word of God everywhere.

Dr Sinclair B. Ferguson,
St George's-Tron Parish Church,
Glasgow

Preaching the Living Word

Christian Focus

ISBN 1 85792 312 x

Published in 1999
by
Christian Focus Publications,
Geanies House, Fearn, Ross-shire,
Scotland, IV20 1TW, Great Britain.

Cover design by Owen Daily

CONTENTS

CONTRIBUTORS

R. C. Lucas
Dick Lucas is Chairman of the Proclamation Trust and was formerly Rector of St. Helens, Bishopsgate, London, for 37 years. He is the author of *Fulness and Freedom: The Message of Colossians*.

J I Packer
Dr. Jim Packer was Professor of Systematic and Historical Theology at Regent College, Vancouver, Canada, having been Vice Principal of Trinity College, Bristol. He is a world-wide speaker and author of many books including *Knowing God* and *Fundamentalism and the Word of God*.

Bruce Milne
Bruce Milne is Senior Minister of First Baptist Church, Vancouver. Born in Scotland, he became Professor of Biblical and Historical Theology and Christian Ethics at Spurgeon's College, London. He is the author of *Know the Truth* and *Here is Your King: The Message of John*.

Alec Motyer
Alec Motyer was formerly Principal of Trinity College Bristol and Vicar of Christ Church, Westbourne, Bournemouth. He is the Old Testament Editor of *The Bible Speaks Today* series of commentaries and the author of many books including *After Death* (Christian Focus), *Look to the Rock* and commentaries on Isaiah and Amos.

Mark Ashton
Mark Ashton is Vicar of St. Andrew The Great Church in Cambridge. He served as a curate in Beckenham, a chaplain at Winchester College and for 6 years as Secretary of the Church Youth Fellowships Association before moving to Cambridge.

Peter Jensen
Dr. Peter Jensen is Principal of Moore Theological College, Sydney, Australia. He is the author of *At the Heart of the Universe*, a handbook on Christian belief.

David Jackman

David Jackman directs the Cornhill Training Course, a one-year, full-time training course for Bible teachers in London. He was formerly senior minister at Above Bar Church in Southampton. He is the author of several books, including *The Message of John's Letters* and, for Christian Focus, *The Authentic Church*, *Taking Jesus Seriously*, and *Understanding the Church*.

Dates when addresses were delivered:
R. C. Lucas – a summary of addresses given at EMA 1997
J. I. Packer – EMA 1991
Bruce Milne – EMA 1994
Alec Motyer – originally given to a meeting of theological students (no date)
Mark Ashton – EMA 1994
Peter Jensen – EMA 1995
David Jackman, Church for the 21st century – EMA 1998
David Jackman, 'Jeremiah 23:23' – EMA 1996

Foreword

Many of the prophecies about 1984 made by George Orwell in his famous book of that title have mercifully not been fulfilled, though his penetrating observations about the drift of late twentieth century western culture remain chillingly trenchant. What 1984 did produce, however, was a new initiative, among ministers and Christian workers in the UK, which under God's hand has developed and flourished, on an annual basis, ever since. June 1984 saw the first Evangelical Ministry Assembly held at St Helen's, Bishopsgate, in the City of London, under the chairmanship of Dick Lucas, then its rector.

Now, as we stand at the end of the century and the beginning of the third Christian millennium, we look back over the fifteen assemblies already held, which for many have become such a valuable and stimulating 'watering hole', in the midst of busy lives and demanding ministries. This volume is by way of a 'taster' of some of the best of EMA over those years, and its publication is timed to coincide with the sixteenth such occasion, in June 1999.

In April 1984, writing his original letter of invitation to the first assembly, Dick Lucas commented on the surprise of some of his friends at seeing him in the role of a conference organiser. There had been several areas of 'pressure', to which he had now 'succumbed'. Firstly, for three years past, he had been holding residential preaching conferences for students and young ministers, which were now in increasing demand. The assembly would provide a daily afternoon preaching school, consisting of 'expositions, analyses of past failures and present dilemmas, as well as instruction in handling the Word of God, not deceitfully, but rightly'. These were to be complemented by a series of morning lectures by Dr Jim Packer on the subject 'True Catholicity in Ministry and Worship'. So, the pattern of a distinguished visiting speaker on a particular doctrinal or ministry theme, combined with Dick's own 'expositions for expositors', became established as the backbone of the new assembly, from the very start. Lady Elizabeth Catherwood and John Blanchard were the additional speakers that first year.

The rest of the letter explained the current need to 'take a stand' for truth, especially in the light of contemporary pressures 'all squeezing us into a mould that should be unacceptable to the renewed Christian mind'. The list was detailed – materialism, ecumenism, secularized theology, behavioural sciences and fanaticism. Yet the way ahead was not ultimately to mobilize our forces to try to fight on each and every front, but 'a recovery of a renewed preaching ministry in the churches'. Calling those who received the letter to turn aside from a multitude of other activities, to give themselves to prayer and the ministry of the Word, Dick concluded that the New Testament recipe for healthy evangelism and church growth was 'apt teachers, full of the Spirit, full of boldness, full of zeal, with the Word of God dwelling richly in them, to be found everywhere and at all times committed wholly to the apostolic task of Prayer and Preaching (Acts 6:2-4)'.

Just over 100 people attended for the three days of that first assembly. In their comments afterwards, the Biblical emphasis and quality of the material were highlighted, as were the welcome, the timekeeping, the lack of 'padding', the good fellowship and the ever popular boxed lunches! We hope that none of those distinctives has been lost over the years. Certainly, it is remarkable to see how strongly those original emphases have been preserved, as the assembly has grown. Indeed, it was numerical growth that moved us to the Central Hall, Westminster, before the IRA bomb struck St Helen's, to which refurbished premises the assembly returned in 1996. With the capacity to seat well over 800, the renewed St Helen's, together with St Andrew's Undershaft, where a huge bookstall now operates, provides a wonderful location in the heart of the City for this annual 'bugle call', as the first assembly was termed (courtesy of the Concise Oxford English Dictionary).

Since then, the Proclamation Trust has been formed, of which the EMA is often regarded as its flagship event. From there, the Cornhill Training Course was founded in 1991 and now trains men and women for Biblical ministry in a widening variety of contexts. The assembly itself has seen the introduction and development of afternoon seminars, on a wide variety of contemporary, ministry-related themes and topics. Each year we have been wonderfully served by our overseas visitors, several of whose contributions feature in this collection. Friends from Australia, Canada, South Africa and the USA have brought us God's Word with clarity and penetration, and through it all the regular Biblical expositions, by Dick Lucas, have run as a rich seam, which many have said would have been worth the three days' investment on their own. But there was so much more....

Perhaps most significant of all has been the EMA's contribution to the cause of evangelical unity, that is not only the 'unity of the Spirit', which we are eager to maintain, but also the 'unity of the faith', which we are equally eager to attain. After the regrettable divisions between Anglican and Free Church evangelicals in the late 1960s and beyond, EMA has consistently sought to bring conservative evangelical Christians together, to take counsel and encourage one another, in the work of the gospel. At the end of the century, those barriers are happily breaking down all around us. The fellowship enjoyed at EMA is becoming much more a norm of Christian experience elsewhere, for which we thank God and take courage.

It is our hope and prayer that this selection of EMA addresses will do more than give a flavour of the annual June assembly. For those who were privileged to hear them when they were first delivered, as well as for those who have not yet attended an EMA, we trust that this clear teaching of the message of Scripture and its application to the contemporary world and church, in all their need, will nurture and motivate a commitment to gospel ministry that is understood, uncompromised and unashamed.

More details of taped EMA addresses and forthcoming Proclamation Trust events (including EMA) can always be requested from Willcox House, 140-148 Borough High Street, London SE1 1LB (Tel: 0171 407 0561). We look forward to hearing from you.

David Jackman
Co-Chairman EMA
London, January 1999

MORE THAN CONQUERORS?
An introduction to Romans 8

R. C. Lucas

1

MORE THAN CONQUERORS?
An introduction to Romans 8

R. C. Lucas

In 1674 Mr Thomas Parker, bookseller, had two shops in London, one 'The Bible and Three Crowns' in Cheapside, and the other, simply 'The Bible', on London Bridge. In that year he published a weighty commentary on Romans 8 with the stately title 'Forty six sermons upon the whole Eighth Chapter of the Epistle of the Apostle Paul to the Romans'. These sermons, Mr Parker informs us, were 'lately preached by the Reverend and Learned Thomas Horton, Doctor in Divinity, and late Minister of Saint Helen's in London'. My copy of this fine commentary was given me from her father's library by Lady Catherwood. Alas! As Minister of St Helen's over 37 years I was never able to provide for that patient morning congregation a series of suitable length on this justly famous chapter. I fear that Dr Horton would have regarded as miserably scrappy the five sermons that I did preach on Romans 8. What then would he say of a bold/rash attempt at EMA 1997 to re-introduce these marvellous 39 verses in just two hour-long sessions, let alone the drastic shortening and re-casting of my material that I am now practising for this EMA collection?

Horton's method, long standing in his day, was to take one verse (sometimes less) for each weekly sermon. The risk inherent in this practice is the possibility of missing the forest for the trees. Normally, an expository series is the better for an introduction, or preliminary overview, to enable the listener, and preacher, to know where they are going, at least in general terms, whatever new treasures are discovered on the journey. In the case of Romans 8, it is particularly important to know what the chapter is about, since so many false signposts exist. For many years, in my lifetime, Romans 8 has been seen as the breaking of the dawn after the darkness and gloom of Romans 7. It is suggested that at this point in his argument the Apostle brings to a defeated Christian news of 'a new and wonderful life' through the fulness of the Spirit's power, a power hitherto unknown. Here at last, it is said, is the secret of Christian 'sanctification', in the sense of an experience of victorious living in which sin is finally mastered. Even more daring, the claim is made that here is the promised 'Full Salvation', available to all those, but only to those, with faith to avail themselves of it.

The *raison d'être* of Romans 8 is almost the exact opposite of this. Paul is writing to Christians already aware of the 'new way of the Spirit' (7:6), already enjoying the outpouring of the Holy Spirit into their hearts (5:5). They knew full well that Christ has won the victory over Sin and Death, and that liberation from these grim old masters was promised in the gospel. But the reality of experience could not be denied by honest believers. Indwelling sin still very easily entangled them. And with regard to the actual pains and perplexities of dying, they seemed no better off than their pagan neighbours: in the local mortuary you would be hard put to discern any difference between the children of this world and the heirs of the Kingdom.

It was precisely in these areas that Christian assurance was so badly shaken. They had been taught that freedom from the law of sin and death was theirs (verse 2). Yet they still sinned; and they still died! In their undoubted and continuing weakness how could they be sure that they were indeed children of God? Why were such bitter trials and tribulations permitted to be their lot? Was God really working for their good? Often there seemed substantial evidence to disprove any such idea. How could you continue to believe that God loved you when unrelenting conflict, within and without, was your experience? In fact, in the darkest hour, there were those who had begun to doubt if they belonged to Christ at all. Was it, after all, an empty dream?

To meet these agonising questionings Paul writes to the Christian believers about their present experience in Christ, and the future expectations that were properly theirs. While the NIV paragraph headings claim no authority, I am content to accept them. First we consider 'Life through the Spirit' (1-17), followed by 'Future Glory' (18-30). Finally, in verses 31-39 the Christians in Rome discover reason to believe that 'God is for them', despite all their defeats, their despairs, and their difficulties. Through the apostle's mighty arguments they come to see that in 'All things' God is working for their good (28) and in 'All things' they can consider themselves to be 'more than conquerors' (37). Glorious assurance indeed!

Section 1 (1-4): Justification and the Gift of the Spirit

These four verses summarize the blessing of 'Righteousness through Faith', a theme Paul has been explaining, and thoroughly exploring, since 3:21. However, the condensed nature of these verses, and the unusual terminology, have led some to suppose that, at this point, a new dimension of Christian living and experience is being offered to the believer, baffled by the relentless demands of indwelling sin. According to this popular interpretation, Romans 8 becomes a second gospel, not this time good news of Christ for sinners, but good news now of the Spirit for 'saints', conscious as they are of many defeats and failures.

To correct this serious misconception I have, on occasion, when reading this chapter with a friend, adopted a practice that has proved enlightening. First, we read 1-4, omitting 2 and 4b; this demonstrates beyond argument that we are here face to face with a summary of the authentic biblical gospel. Here is the glorious message of what God has done in sending his own Son to die as a sin-offering, thus meeting all the

righteous demands of the law. Justification, since it is the
verdict of the Last Day, is more than pardon for sins past. It
means that all the requirements of the law, laid upon us until
our lives' end, are met by the obedience of Christ. Without
this there never could be the possibility, even for the mature
Christian advanced in holy living, of enjoying the privileges
of 'no condemnation', since the most godly believer must
often echo the words of the Psalm 19:12, 'Who can tell how
often he offends? O cleanse me from my hidden (i.e.
unrecognised) faults'.

Needless to say, from Paul's time onwards this teaching
has caused alarm (Rom. 6:1, 15). What reckless antinomi-
anism is this! What licence to sin! Promised such a verdict
at the end, will we not inevitably lead careless lives in the
present?

But for one vital, easily forgotten, factor this protest would
stand. So, clear now about the problem, my friend and I read
verses 1-4 again, omitting nothing! Here we meet Paul's
normal teaching, that with justification comes, always and
necessarily, the gift of the Spirit. The essential link is in
Romans 5:1-5 (cp. Tit. 3:5b, 6). And has this not been the
teaching of Romans 6 as well, that those who share in the
benefits of Christ's death, share also in the power of his
resurrection?

Verses 1-4, then, bring together what in New Testament
teaching on Christian initiation is never separated (cp. Acts
19:1f.), namely that the work of God 'for us' through Christ
is always witnessed in our experience by the work of God
'in us' by his Spirit. This is the normal Christian life as, by
God's grace, it begins. Only those who live 'according to
the Spirit' can claim that justification is theirs. 'No
condemnation' is not simply a doctrinal conviction; the
assurance of this freedom from the reign of sin and death is
written in our hearts, and demonstrated by us, in the 'new
way of the Spirit' (6:6). But what are the hallmarks of this
New Way?

Section 2 (5-8): Regeneration and the Power of the Spirit
These verses spell out a dramatic contrast, not between a beaten and bewildered Christian on the one hand, and a Spirit-filled believer on the other. The comparison is between those who are regenerate and those who are not. If it seems that the unregenerate get the lion's share of this section it must be to demonstrate just how deep was the pit from which the believer has been rescued. What the apostle centres on here is the 'inner citadel' of every person, namely the mind, or mind-set. This refers to those deepest desires that define us for what we are. Verse 5 sets out, with the profoundest simplicity, the great change that regeneration brings about. The natural person, however educated or refined, must live by natural desires, which, as spelt out in Romans chapters 1–3, are fallen; Jew and Gentile alike are all under the power of sin (3:9ff.)

But now through the power of the indwelling Spirit, the believer is liberated from the dominion of self-seeking, and finds instead a newly awakened ambition to set mind and heart on what God's Spirit desires. The road to destruction has been decisively rejected for the road that leads to life (verse 6). Also, now left behind are those grim evidences of an unregenerate life, hostility to God, refusal to submit to the divine sovereignty, and inability to please God in any way (verses 7,8). By the miracle of regeneration the Spirit has taken control of the citadel! The old management has received notice to quit. All things are now new. However, is this wonderful description true of me?

Section 3 (9-11): Resurrection and the Indwelling of the Spirit
In these verses Paul applies the teaching thus far to his particular readers. He reassures these halting believers as to their spiritual standing, shaken as they have been by the persistent and painful evidences that indwelling sin, far from lying down defeated, is determined to reclaim the inner

citadel. Despite grievous disloyalty in listening so readily
to their sinful nature, Paul's readers may be confident in their
Christian standing by the fact that the Spirit remains with
them. The hallmark of belonging to Christ is the indwelling
Spirit.

It is interesting to see that Paul refuses to distinguish here
between the indwelling Spirit and 'Christ in you'. There is
no suggestion that those who have Christ in the heart may yet
not have an experience of the indwelling Spirit of God. So
far from Paul's understanding is this popular error, that he
can write, in Romans 8, that those who do not have 'life
through the Spirit', as explained in this chapter, are not
Christians at all (verse 9)!

The great value of this section lies in the clarity with
which Paul teaches Christians what is ours now in this world,
and what will be ours only, but certainly, in the world to
come.

Now (verse 10), we have in our bodies the sentence of
death because of sin. Our mortality remains; we do not yet
experience the redemption of our bodies (verse 23). But the
risen life of Christ is ours nonetheless – we are already risen
with Christ (Col. 3:1). Because of 'righteousness', that is to
say justification and no condemnation, we have the life of
the Spirit within. We are 'alive in Christ' by the power of
his Spirit. This 'life' now drives our deepest ambitions, as
we saw in verses 5-8, so different from the ways of the old
life.

But though our mortal bodies must die, that is not the end
of the matter (verse 11). The same Spirit of God who raised
Jesus from the dead, will raise his people from the grave,
granting them a resurrection body such as their Saviour
displayed to his apostles on that first Easter Day. And the
Assurance of this is given us now by the indwelling Spirit
(cp. Eph. 1:13, 14).

However, if the new believer is marked by the indwelling
Spirit, and if indwelling sin is the mark of my mortality, will

the Christian life not be one of constant conflict within? And to which of these powerful forces should I listen?

Section 4 (12-17): Sonship and the Leading of the Spirit

The fight is on (cp Gal. 5:16-26)! But the believer now has an obligation to be led by the Spirit, not the sinful nature. The old way of living according to the sinful nature leads only to death, and would be totally incongruous for the regenerate who 'serves in the new way of the Spirit'(6:6). How then does the Spirit invariably lead the child of God? The fascinating answer to this question is that he leads us vigorously to turn our backs on sin, and to turn ourselves not so much towards goodness as towards God our Father. The misdeeds, inevitably arising from the sinful nature while we remain in this mortal body, are to be mortified, or put to death, a daily dying to the claims of evil. At the same time as the Spirit enables us to draw decisively away from sin each day, he draws us powerfully to our Father, to whom we continuously pray. It is precisely this daily renunciation of the 'misdeeds of the body' and this daily approach to God, that reassures us of our standing as part of God's family, and confirms to us that the Spirit is at work within us. For what a great power it must be to encourage within us such persistent repentance and faith! This is the leading of the Spirit.

But can we claim to be led by the power of the Spirit, and yet remain so weak, experience so much frustration, and be hard pressed on every side (cp 2 Cor 4:7f.)? And was it not just the experiences listed in verse 35b that caused Paul's critics to doubt his credentials as an apostle of Christ?

Section 5 (18-27): Suffering and the Help of the Spirit

This remarkable paragraph looks at the present and compares it with the future. In the 'present sufferings' Paul lists the sighs, or groanings, of creation (18-22), the Christian (23-25), and the Spirit within us (26, 27). The future is variously described as 'the glorious freedom of the children of God'

(21), the 'redemption of our bodies' (23) and the 'conformity of believers into 'the likeness of Christ' (29).

First, the whole created order must wait (eagerly!) for the Day when God's children are revealed, finally liberated from indwelling sin and death. Meanwhile the creation, or cosmos, is marked by its bondage to decay.

Secondly, the believing Christian longs (eagerly!) for the Day when the body is finally redeemed in the resurrection, and the glorious freedom of the children of God experienced. This is our Christian hope – full salvation.

Thirdly, the Spirit sighs as he intercedes for us, knowing both our present weaknesses and God's will for his people's future glory. How great the distance between now and then! We do not even know the immensity of God's purposes for his saints. But the Spirit knows! Can the evil principalities and powers withstand such intercession or deny its certain answer? What assurance then is ours!

Section 6 (28-30): God's Sovereign Will

God's will is that his Son should be the 'firstborn among many brothers'. To that end it is a divine necessity that the elect should be 'conformed to the likeness of his Son' (verse 29). To this end it is ordained that we, who will share in Christ's glory, should share also in his sufferings (verse 17). These sufferings comprise the 'all things' of verse 28. To all appearances they are the very opposite of all that we would call 'good'. But we know otherwise. In all the agonies of this present age, where sin reigns in death (Rom. 5:12-21), God is at work for the real good of those who love him, beginning his activity in the believer's life before birth and bringing it to completion after death. The irresistible progress by which the will of God takes its course is exceedingly impressive. So certain is it that we shall be glorified that Paul speaks of this marvellous consummation as though it is already achieved (verse 30). But are there no supernatural powers, beyond our ken, able to frustrate these purposes? Read on!

Section 7 (31-39): God's Sovereign Love

These verses make a grand conclusion, known for its sublime eloquence and memorable certainties. But more than rhetoric is here. It is 'all business' as Paul restores and builds up the assurance of his readers. For the reality, wonderfully spelt out, is that no-one in all creation can condemn the one whom God has justified. Nor can any trouble or tragedy separate us from the solid certainty and conviction of the love of Christ for us.

It is important to see that the reality of death has, all through, been at the forefront of the Christians' perplexities, as is clear from verse 35, verse 36 (where the Old Testament reference describes the sense of abandonment by God that undeserved, or untimely, death so often produces), and verse 37, where death takes unexpected precedence over life.

So we come to Paul's final conviction that in 'all these things' that appear to spell out the reign of sin and death, we, who are called according to God's purposes, are, by faith and hope, more than conquerors indeed. 'And hope does not disappoint us, because God has poured out his love into our hearts by the Holy Spirit whom he has given us' (Rom. 5:5).

Note
Many able and stimulating commentaries on Romans continue to appear, with the result that fine older commentators may be overlooked. Two such are, for me, quite indispensable; Hodge on Romans (the Banner of Truth reprint includes the essential Doctrine Notes and Remarks), and the Lutheran Anders Nygren on Romans, whose brilliant insights supplement Hodge (English edition 1952, and reprints). Among smaller commentaries on Romans I have long valued *The Power of God* by James Philip, with a foreword by Sinclair Ferguson (Gray Publishing, Glasgow).

FROM THE SCRIPTURES
TO THE SERMON

J.I. Packer

2

SOME PERSPECTIVES ON PREACHING

J. I. Packer

'I urge you, Timothy, as we live in the sight of God and of
Christ Jesus (whose coming in power will judge the living
and the dead), to preach the Word of God. Never lose your
sense of urgency, in season or out of season. Prove, correct,
and encourage, using the utmost patience in your teaching.'
Thus J.B. Phillips, that prince of paraphrasts, renders the
first two verses of 2 Timothy 4. Note the aspects of the
communicative action that Paul prescribes (they are all there
in the Greek): proclamation, demonstration, correction,
instruction. Note the commitment to the preaching ministry
for which Paul calls: press on, he says, with utmost urgency
and stick-to-it-ive-ness (a fine North American word that
catches the force of *makrothumia* better than does the English
scholar's 'patience'). And now consider whether we
evangelicals, who so often cite these words of Paul to each
other and who claim to know so clearly that the preaching of
the Word is the power-source of the church, can be said to
succeed in rising to the demands of this insight that we inherit.
It must be admitted that often we fail here; we do not succeed
in preaching the Word of God as plainly, pungently and
powerfully as we would like to do. What follows is offered
in the hope that it will help us to preach better. If you do not
find my thoughts useful, please remember that, like so many
unsuccessful sermons, they were at least well meant.

1. A theological and functional focus for preaching
First, let me focus the concept of preaching the Word of God
as I think it ought to be focused. I do not define preaching

institutionally or sociologically, but theologically and functionally. An institutional definition would present preaching in terms of buildings, pulpits and pews.[1] A sociological definition would view preaching as a special kind of monologue fulfilling specific corporate expectations on the part of the group being addressed. Both types of definition are no doubt useful in their place; but if one is, or hopes to be, a preacher oneself, and wants to know what is involved in fulfilling the ministry that Paul urged upon Timothy, then what one needs is a theological definition that shows what should happen when preaching takes place.

Christian preaching is *the event of God himself bringing to an audience a Bible-based, Christ-related, life-impacting message of instruction and direction through the words of a spokesperson.* Please note the following four points about this definition. Firstly, it is *theological*: it conceptualizes preaching in terms not of human performance but of divine communication. Secondly, it is *prophetic*: it views God as speaking his own message via a messenger whose sole aim is to receive and relay what God gives. Thirdly, it is *incarnational*: it envisages God embodying his communication in the person of the messenger who both delivers it and, in delivering it, models response to it. Phillips Brooks' famous delineation of preaching as truth through personality[2] points to the way in which personal attitudes to God and man come through in the course of declaring God's message. The demeanour of preachers in their messenger-role as bearers of God's truth and wisdom to people whom God loves will always, for better or for worse, become part of their message and affect the impact that they make. Jesus himself, God's incarnate Son, is the paradigm case here. Finally, this normative definition of preaching has a *critical* function to fulfil, for it obliges us to test pulpit utterances, and to say of any that was not Bible-based, Christ-related and life-impacting, that, whatever else it was, it was not preaching in the full and proper meaning of that word.

Preaching as described is necessary for a healthy church. Without a regular diet of Bible-based, Christ-related, life-impacting messages from God the mind-set of a congregation will become either institutionalist and sacramentalist, as in old-style Roman Catholicism where there was not effective preaching, or moralistic and legalistic, as in liberal Protestant congregations where the agenda is social service and God is expected to accept one for doing it. Where there is preaching of the type described, however, the Bible will be received.

So I do not equate preaching with what is called sermonizing or pulpiteering. Not every performance from the preacher's podium is preaching. Some sermonizing produces only bitter wisecracks about the pulpit as coward's castle, and preachers as standing six feet above contradiction, talking at rather than to their hearers, and as climaxing invisibility during the week with incomprehensibility on Sunday, and so on. But such sermonizing, which is certainly bad preaching, by my definition may not be preaching at all, though the institutional and sociological definitions would compel us to call it that. From my theological standpoint, what is said from the pulpit is only preaching if its content conforms to the specification stated above. Conversely, any communication that fulfils these specifications ought to be categorized as preaching, wherever and however it is done – as when Philip sat in the Ethiopian eunuch's chariot and 'told him the good news about Jesus' (Acts 8:35, NIV); (The King James Version has 'preached unto him Jesus'; the Greek word is *euangelizomai*, one of the two main New Testament terms for declaring the gospel). For the New Testament, a Christian spokesman preaches (*kerussō*) only when some aspect of the God-given message concerning Christ (the *kerugma*) is the content of the utterance. This is not our usual modern way of looking at the matter, but it is the biblical way, and it is always best to follow the Bible.

Preaching regards the Bible as the Word of God, because

it will constantly be impacting people as just that; Jesus Christ will be known and loved, because he will constantly be projected as lover and Saviour of our souls; and Christians will grow and flourish through being fed on true spiritual food. Surely it is beyond dispute that a church made and kept healthy by authentic preaching must ever be our goal.

2. Difficulties obstructing the way of faithful preaching
Today's evangelicalism has behind it a noble heritage of preaching. The Reformation itself grew out of practical biblical preaching with Christ at the centre. The great Puritan movement (and it was great) was sustained on both sides of the Atlantic by preaching of this kind. The eighteenth-century revival in Britain and the Great Awakening in New England were profound spiritual movements with powerful evangelical preaching at their heart. In the nineteenth century men like C. H. Spurgeon sustained magnificent ministries by preaching in this fashion, and, more recently, men like Donald Barnhouse and Martyn Lloyd-Jones have done the same. But the great tradition is currently tapering off. Why is this? we ask. What has happened to eclipse the grand-scale presentations of the works, ways and will of God, through which evangelicalism once grew lively and strong? It is not that preachers as a body have stopped caring about preaching or trying to do it properly; the problem goes deeper, and arises in the first instance from the drift of our culture. We live in days in which the credibility of faithful biblical preaching is radically doubted, not only outside but inside the churches as well. Also, misguided but insistent expectations on the part of the listeners put many difficulties in the way of faithful preaching that were not there before. Five factors in particular operate in this way; we need to be aware of them, so what follows is a review of them.

Firstly, *the prevalence of non-preaching in Christian pulpits has eroded awareness of what true preaching is.*

Lack of good models always tends to lower standards, and unfortunately good models have been in short supply throughout this century. Far too many pulpit discourses have been put together on wrong principles. Some have failed to open up Scripture; some have expounded biblical doctrine without applying it, thus qualifying as lectures rather than preachments (for lecturing aims only to clear the head, while preaching seeks to change the life); some have been no more than addresses focusing the present self-awareness of the listeners, but not at any stage confronting them with the Word of God; some have been mere statements of the preacher's opinion, based solely on his own expertise, rather than messages from God carrying divine authority. Such discourses are less than preaching, as was stated previously, but because they were announced as sermons they are treated as preaching and people's idea of preaching gets formed in terms of them, so that the true conception of preaching is forgotten.

It is often said, and truly, that sermons must teach Bible truth, and that the renewal of preaching needed today will take its rise from a fresh awareness that this is so. My slighting reference to some content-laden sermons as lectures rather than preachments may therefore have seemed perplexing. But preaching is more than teaching – not less, but more! Preaching is essentially teaching plus application (invitation, direction, summons), and where that plus is lacking something less than preaching takes place. Study of printed sermons from past generations reveals that older evangelical preachers kept a careful balance between doctrinal content as such (biblical orthodoxy) and practical and experiential applications (biblical orthopraxy) – something like half and half in most messages. In our day, however, the balance has been largely lost, and sermons tend to be either all doctrinal content without application, or all exhortation without doctrinal content; and to the extent to which either form of imbalance prevails, both types of

utterance become instances of non-preaching, and very
inadequate models, therefore, of what preaching ought to be.
Many in our churches have never experienced preaching of
the historic evangelical sort at all.

Secondly, *topical as distinct from textual preaching has
become common in North America (less so in Britain and
elsewhere).*

For sermons to explore announced themes rather than
biblical passages is a twentieth-century development, and
hardly a happy one. It has occurred, partly at least, to make
preaching appear interesting and important to a generation
that largely has lost interest in the pulpit; partly, no doubt, to
make the sermon seem different from what goes on in a Bible
class; and partly, too, because many topical preachers do
not trust their Bible enough to let it speak for itself and utter
its own message through their lips. Whatever the reasons,
the results are unhealthy. In a topical sermon any text taken
is reduced to a peg on which the speaker hangs his own line
of thought. The shape and thrust of his message thus reflect
no more than his own idea of what is good for people, and
then the only authority that the sermon can have is the human
authority of a knowledgeable person speaking with emphasis
(raising his voice, perhaps, and even banging the pulpit). To
my mind, topical sermons of this sort, no matter how biblical
their component parts may be, cannot but fall short of being
preaching in the full sense, just because in them the authority
of God speaking is dissolved, more or less, into the authority
of human religious expertise. Many in our churches have
only ever been exposed to topical preaching of this kind: no
wonder then that they do not appreciate what real preaching
might be.

Thirdly, *low expectations become self-fulfilling. Where
little is expected from sermons, little is received.*

Many moderns have never been taught to expect sermons
to matter much, and so their habit at sermon time is to relax,
settle back and wait to see if anything the preacher says will

catch their interest. Most of today's congregations and preachers seem to be at one in neither asking nor anticipating that God will come to meet his people in the preaching; so it is no wonder if this fails to happen. According to your unbelief, we might say, be it unto you! Just as it takes two to tango, so ordinarily it takes an expectant, praying congregation, along with a preacher who knows what he is about, to make an authentic preaching occasion. A century ago in Reformed circles in Britain the regular question to a person coming from church was, how did he or she 'get on' under the preaching of the Word. This reflected the expectancy of which I am speaking. Nowadays, however, on both sides of the Atlantic, the commoner question is, how did the preacher 'get on' in his stated pulpit performance? This shows how interest has shifted and the mental attitude has changed. It is now assumed that those who sit under the preaching are observers, measuring the preacher's performance, rather than participants waiting for the Word of God. Many in our congregations do not know that there is any other way of listening to sermons than this way of detached passivity, and no-one should be surprised to find that those who cultivate such passivity often dismiss preaching as an uneventful bore. Those who seek little find little.

Fourthly, *the power of speech to communicate significance has in our Western culture become suspect, so that any form of oratory, rhetoric, or dramatic emphasis to show the weight and significance of stated facts tends to alienate rather than convince.*

This development is mainly due to the media. On radio and television strong expressions of feeling sound and look hysterical; cool and chatty intimacy is required if one is to communicate successfully. This standard of communicative sincerity is now applied everywhere. Prior to this century a preacher could use words dramatically and emphatically for up to an hour to set forth the majesty of God the King, the glory of Christ the Saviour, the greatness of the soul, the momentous importance of eternity, and the significance of present reactions to the gospel message for determining personal destiny, and congregations appreciated the manner as being appropriate to the matter. Nowadays, that kind of utterance is widely felt to be false, as if passionate speech as such argues a purpose of browbeating and bludgeoning the mind, pulling the wool over the eyes, and carrying through a confidence trick. To avoid this suspicion, many preachers nowadays talk of spiritual life and death in a style better fitted to reading the sports results, and their cosy intimacy makes the theme itself seem trivial or unreal. The discrediting among us of grand-scale public speech puts preachers into what might well be felt to be a no-win situation.

It was my privilege, many years ago, to spend a winter under the preaching ministry of the late Dr. Martyn Lloyd-Jones, and to enjoy a working relationship with him for twenty years after that, so that I was able to observe from many angles his approach to the preacher's task. His gifts fitted him for grand-scale ministry, and his sense of spiritual reality told him that great things must be said in a way that projected their greatness. He could fairly be described as a nineteenth-century preacher born out of due time, and though he was fully aware that the older type of preaching had become suspect and unfashionable he continued to practise it and to encourage others to do the same. Combining the electric energy of the orator with the analytical precision of the courtroom or the clinic, and focusing his businesslike rhetoric on the inner drama of the gracious hound of heaven capturing and changing sinners' benighted hearts, he communicated an overwhelming sense of the greatness of God and the weight of spiritual issues. He left behind him a large body of hearers, myself among them, who will for ever be thankful that as a modern man he deliberately swam against the stream and did the old thing.

The vision of preaching that I gained from him, as from no-one else, stays with me, and what I am writing here reflects my experience of the power of preaching under his ministry. From the vantage-point that this experience gave me, I urge that the only real way forward for preachers today is to follow Dr. Lloyd-Jones in cultivating an honesty with words that earns us the right to fly in the face of our laid-back culture and to dwell passionately, urgently, dramatically, and at appropriate length, on the desperately important agenda of the relationship between God and man. In this, as in so much else, the old paths constitute the good way. But how few today, preachers or people, know it!

Fifthly, *spiritual issues themselves, issues of radical repentance, self-despairing faith, costly cross-bearing as central to discipleship, spending and being spent in order to do others good, putting holiness before happiness, and keeping the world out of one's heart, are felt to be irrelevant by many church attenders.*

The problem that preachers face here is that church attendance for many has little or nothing to do with the quest for God. Because church-going is the mark of a respectable and trustworthy citizen; or because attending an appropriate ethnic or denominational church helps keep alive one's cultural heritage; or because the genial and relaxed regularities of Sunday worship help to stabilize a hectic life; or because faithful church-going is thought to guarantee some kind of happy lot in the next world; or because one likes the people one meets at church; and so on. There are many such reasons, but none of them has anything to do with knowing and loving God and none of them, therefore, fosters any spiritual interest in preaching. So when preachers point the way to a richer relationship with God, this type of hearer feels a sense of irrelevance, and his or her heart is inclined to say: 'Here is a religious professional talking about the things he is paid to talk about: I am not a religious professional, so none of that is really my business; however, I will sit through it patiently, as good manners require.' Preachers, for their part, know that this is how many of their hearers are thinking, so they strain every nerve to speak in a way that will lead persons without spiritual interest to rate them fascinating, relevant and smart. How we love to be rated smart! But this preoccupation does not encourage faithful spiritual preaching, and results in congregations not experiencing faithful spiritual preaching for long periods together.

All these factors tend to set up wrong standards and thus constitute obstacles to the kind of preaching that I seek to commend. However, difficulties are there to be overcome; so I proceed.

True authority in preaching

So far I have been clearing the ground for discussion of my main concern in this chapter, which is to show what authority in preaching means and to suggest how it might be re-established in today's churches. My interest at this stage centres not on homiletics, that is, the technical procedures whereby preachers bring to us what they have to tell us about God, but rather on the theology of preaching, that is, the supernatural process whereby God through his messenger brings to us what he has to tell us about himself. Preaching as a work of God, mediating the authority of God, is my theme, and the rest of this chapter will be devoted to its development in a direct way.

The first step in opening up this theme must be to outline what I mean when I refer to the authority of God. Authority is a multi-faceted relationship with a moral and intellectual as well as a governmental side. The basic idea is of a claim to exercise control that is founded on having the right, power and competence to do it. The authority that belongs to God springs from his sovereign dominion over us as his dependent creatures, linked with the moral perfection of all his dealings with us. Holy Scripture, 'God's Word written' (Anglican Article 25), is the instrument of God's authority; our Lord Jesus Christ exercises and embodies it; and the Holy Spirit induces acknowledgment of it by making us realize the reality of the Father and the Son as they address us in all their awesomeness, holiness and graciousness. God speaks through his Word, written and preached, and our preaching of the Word should match the Spirit's strategy – that is, we should always be seeking to bring home God's reality and authority to human minds and hearts by elucidating and applying Holy Scripture. Encounter with the living, authoritative Lord brings spiritual understanding and life as we hear and respond to his call for trust and obedience, praise and worship, and the preacher's aim should ever be to occasion this edifying encounter. The following discussion seeks to show something of what this means, and so to help us set our sights as preachers more effectively.

I ask three questions.

First: *what does it mean for preaching to be marked by authority?*

The answer I propose is that authority in preaching is a reality in every situation in which the following things are true.

(1) There is no doubt about the *nature* of what is happening: *the Bible is doing the talking.* The preacher is treating himself as a mouthpiece for the biblical word of God, and that word is coming through. He has resisted the temptation to stand in front of his text, as it were, speaking for it as if it could not speak for itself, and putting himself between it and the congregation. Instead, he is making it his business to focus everyone's attention on the text, to stand behind it rather than in front of it, to become its servant, and to let it deliver its message through him. As the Westminster Directory for Public Worship put it, three and a half centuries ago, what the preacher presents must be 'contained in or grounded on (his) text, *that the hearers may discern how God teacheth it from thence*'. Preaching has authority only when the message comes as a word from God himself, and that only happens when what is said is perceived as, in the

words of the Westminster Confession (I.x), 'the Holy Spirit speaking in the Scripture,' and that perception only occurs as the preacher labours to let the text talk through him about that with which, like every other text in the Bible, it is ultimately dealing – God and man in relationship, one way or another. If what is presented appears as the preacher's ideas, it can have only human authority at best; when, however, the preacher serves the written Word in a way that lets it speak for itself, its divine authority is felt.

(2) There is no doubt about the purpose of what is happening: *response to God is being called for*. The preacher, as spokesman for the text, is seeking not only to inform and persuade, but to evoke an appropriate answer to what God through the text is saying and showing. Man's answer will consist of repentance, faith, obedience, love, effort, hope, fear, zeal, joy, praise, prayer, or some blend of these; for such are the dispositional qualities, springing from the heart into devotional and doxological expression, that God everywhere requires. The preacher is hoping, under God, to reproduce the state of affairs that Paul looked back to when he wrote to the Romans, 'you wholeheartedly obeyed the form of teaching to which you were entrusted' (Rom. 6:17). The teaching is God's testimony, command, and promise; the preacher entrusts his hearers to it by begging them to respond to it and assuring them that God will fulfil his promises to them as they do so; and in this process the divine authority of the message is felt.

(3) There is no doubt about the *perspective* of what is happening: *the preaching is practical*. This point is an extension of the last. What is being said would not be preaching at all were it not life-centred. Communication from the text is preaching only as it is applied and brought to bear on the listeners with a life-changing thrust. Without this, as we noted earlier, it would merely be a lecture – that is, a discourse designed to clear people's heads and stock their minds, but not in any direct way to change their lives.

I must confess that I do not think that the present-day evangelical pulpit is strong here. Reacting against the kind of preaching that too often marks the liberal pulpit, in which the speaker offers personal reflections on human and religious life, too many of us preach messages that suffer from what might be called 'doctrinal overload'. With thirty minutes in which to preach, we spend twenty-eight of them teaching general principles of divine truth from our text, and only for the last minute or two do we engage in any form of application. But there is little sense of God's authority where so much of the message is lecture and so little application is found.

A wiser way of proceeding, and one that mediated a very vivid sense of divine authority, was that followed by Dr. Martyn Lloyd-Jones in the greatest days of his preaching ministry. The introductions to his pastoral and evangelistic sermons were very cunningly conceived. Having announced his text, he would spend the first few minutes of the sermon talking about some widely felt perplexity of modern life, pointing out in everyday language that no adequate solution or remedy seemed to be in sight. In this he was operating on the wise principle, 'scratch where it itches,' and involving his hearers in a realization that this was their problem, pressing and inescapable. When he had secured their interest at this level, he would begin to demonstrate that this text gives God's angle on the problem and his answer to it, and the demonstration would be applicatory all the way. Not everyone who experienced the authority of God in the preaching of 'the Doctor' discerned its source. Certainly, Dr. Lloyd-Jones' personal power as a speaker and his humble, insightful submission to his text had much to do with it, but much of the authority flowed from the fact that he was applying the truth in a searchingly practical way throughout to remedy the need that he had already brought his hearers to face and own. The more explicit the practical perspective, and the more overtly it involves the listeners, the more the divine authority of the preaching will be felt.

(4) There is no doubt about the impact of what is happening: *the presence and power of God are being experienced.* The preaching mediates an encounter not merely with truth, but with God himself. A staggering throwaway line in 1 Corinthians 14 illustrates this. Paul is showing the superior usefulness of prophecy (speaking God's message in intelligible language) over tongues, and he says: '... if the whole church comes together and everyone speaks in tongues, and some who do not understand or some unbelievers come in, will they not say that you are out of your mind?' (Expected answer: Yes.) 'But if an unbeliever or someone who does not understand comes in while everybody is prophesying, he will be convinced by all that he is a sinner and will be judged by all, and the secrets of his heart will be laid bare. So he will fall down and worship God, exclaiming, "God is really among you!"' (1 Cor. 14:23-25). Whatever else in this passage is uncertain, four things at least are plain. First, prophecy as Paul speaks of it here corresponds in content to what we would call preaching the gospel: detecting sin, and announcing God's remedy. Second, the expected effect of such prophecy was to create a sense of being in the presence of the God of whom it spoke, and of being searched and convicted by him, and so being moved to humble oneself and worship him. Third, in the experience of both Paul and the Corinthians, what Paul describes must have actually occurred, otherwise he could not have expected the Corinthians to believe his assertion; for that which never happened before cannot be predicted with such certainty. Fourth, Paul is anticipating a situation in which a divine authority in and through the preaching would be felt.

To sum up, then: preaching is marked by authority when the message is a relaying of what is taught by the text, when active response to it is actively sought, when it is angled in a practical, applicatory way that involves the listeners' lives, and when God himself is encountered through it. So much for the first question.

Secondly: *what are the hindrances to authority in our preaching?*

Lack of a clearly Bible-based, applicatory message, summoning its hearers one way or another to a deeper relationship with God in Christ, precludes the possibility of authority.

Imprecision, confusion, and muddle in presentation, so that the message and its application cannot be grasped clearly, has the same effect.

Self-projection also undermines and erodes authority. If by his words and manner the preacher focuses attention on himself, thus modelling some mode of self-absorption or self-satisfaction rather than humble response to the word that he proclaims, he precludes all possibility of his channelling any sense of divine authority; what he does not feel himself he cannot mediate to others. James Denney said that you cannot convey the impression both that you are a great preacher and that Jesus Christ is a great Saviour; he might have added: or that the Lord is a great God. God-projection and Christ-projection rather than self-projection is the way to communicate and engender in one's hearers a sense of divine authority in one's preaching.

Self-reliance in the act of preaching is a further hindrance to true authority in preaching. Like self-projection, it too has the effect of inducing the hearers to attend to the messenger rather than the message – in other words, to man rather than to God – and authentic authority is eliminated when that happens.

So to my final question.

Thirdly: *what are the conditions of authority in our preaching?*

To this question I offer first a general and then a specific answer.

The general answer is that preaching has authority when both its substance and its style proclaim in a transparent way the preacher's own docile humility before the Bible itself and before the triune God whose word the Bible is. It is as the preacher himself is truly under, and is seen clearly to be under, the authority of God and the Bible that he will have authority, and be felt to carry authority, as God's spokesman. It needs to be obvious to the hearers that he has put himself wholeheartedly under the authority of God as whose emissary he comes; of Christ the chief shepherd, whom he serves as a subordinate shepherd, and to whom he must one day give account of his service; and of the Holy Spirit, whom he trusts each moment as he preaches to communicate the divine message to his hearers' hearts at that moment. A preacher who has authority will come across as one who consciously depends on the Holy Spirit to sustain in him vividness of vision, clarity of mind and words, and freedom of heart and voice, as he delivers his message, just as he trusts the Holy Spirit to be the agent of conviction and response in the lives of his hearers. It is those under authority who have authority; it is those whose demeanour models submission to the Scriptures and dependence on the Lord of the Word who mediate the experience of God's authority in preaching. 'Unlike so many,' writes Paul, 'we do not peddle the word of God for profit' – that is, we do not preach with mercenary motives, nor do we modify the message in order to please hearers who, if pleased, will smile on us, but if displeased, might become obnoxious to us. 'On the contrary, in Christ we speak before God with sincerity, like men sent from God' (2 Cor. 2:17). Only those preachers who could say the same, by reason of their conscious and conscientious fidelity to the written Word, are likely ever to be able to say, as Paul elsewhere said: 'we also thank God continually because, when you received the word of God, which you heard from us, you accepted it not as the word of men, but as it actually is, the word of God, which is at work in you who believe' (1 Thess. 2:13).

Conditions of authority

Specifically, and looking at the matter directly from our own standpoint as preachers, the conditions of authority are four in number, each of which we should recognize as a summons and a directive to us from the Lord himself.

Firstly, the heart of our message on each occasion must be an application of biblical material to the heart and conscience, to lead people to know, love, worship and serve God through Jesus Christ. Is this our constant purpose when we preach?

Secondly, the way we preach must display a transparent wholeheartedness of response to our own message, as well as thorough commitment to persuade our hearers to trust, love, honour and serve the Lord as we ourselves seek to do. Constant self-scrutiny is therefore required of preachers in particular, to make sure that our own hearts are right before we attempt to speak in the Lord's name. Do we practise this self-scrutiny?

Thirdly, we need the unction of the Holy Spirit for the act of preaching itself.[3] Richard Baxter, the Puritan, in his classic volume, *The Reformed Pastor* (which every would-be pastor-preacher will be wise to read once a year), spoke of 'a communion of souls' that takes place in preaching, whereby the hearers catch the preacher's mood.[4] This being so, it is vital that the preacher should be full of the Holy Spirit for his appointed task, so that he is clear-headed, warm-hearted, ardent, earnest, and inwardly free to concentrate on the task of instruction and persuasion that each message imposes. An anointing of the Spirit, therefore, giving *parrhēsia* – uninhibited freedom to say from one's heart what one sees with one's heart – is to be sought every time we preach. Beethoven wrote on the score of his *Missa Sollennis* (Mass in D, op. 126): 'From the heart it comes, to the heart may it go,' and these same words should express the preacher's desire every time he ventures to speak. But it is only as we seek and receive the divine unction, sermon by sermon, that it will be so. Do we seek unction as we should?

Finally, we need grace to be spontaneous when we preach: by which I mean, easy and free-flowing in appropriate expression. This, too, is a gift from God – it is an aspect of the *parrhēsia* that the Spirit bestows – but it does not come without hard work in preparation: preparation not just of the message but also, and even primarily, of the messenger. The appropriate formula here comes, I believe, from W.H. Griffith Thomas, and runs as follows: 'Think yourself empty; read yourself full; write yourself clear; pray yourself keen; then into the pulpit – and let yourself go!' That is the sort of preparation that produces spontaneity. Is this how we prepare to preach?

May God bless us all in our preaching ministry, and empower us to preach with authority – as we ought to preach!

Notes

1. Most books on preaching assume an institutional definition. Typical is this, from D. Martyn Lloyd-Jones: 'What then is preaching? What do I mean by preaching? Let us look at it like this. There, is a man standing in a pulpit and speaking, and there, are people sitting in pews or seats and listening. What is happening? Why is this? Why does that man stand in the pulpit? What is his object? Why does the Church put him there to do this? Why do these other people come to listen? What is this man meant to be doing? What is he trying to do? What ought he to be doing? These it seems to me are the greatest questions ... (*Preaching and Preachers*, Grand Rapids: Zondervan, 1972, p. 53).

2. 'Preaching is the bringing of truth through personality' (Phillips Brooks, *Lectures on Preaching*, London: H.R. Allenson Ltd., [1877], p. 5).

3. See Lloyd-Jones, *op. cit.*, pp. 304-25.

4. Richard Baxter, *The Reformed Pastor*, London: Banner of Truth, 1974, p. 149.

3

THE PROBLEM OF PARADIGMS

J. I. Packer

The word *paradigm* has become something of a technical term in modern academic discussion.[1] It is used to mean what we would once have called an overall frame of reference, or a controlling point of view. A paradigm is a large-scale hypothesis about reality that is presupposed and taken for granted as a basis for interpreting data and determining values, goals and procedures. One's paradigm determines one's mind-set, shaping one's thinking by giving it direction and establishing boundaries and limits beyond which belief may not go. Paradigms thus exert control, and usually without our realizing what is happening; who, under ordinary circumstances, reflects on how much he or she is taking for granted? So our paradigms of reality determine how we process informational data – what we make of it, to put it in everyday terms – for processing data is essentially a matter of fitting the bits into our overall frame of reference. Thus paradigms become the pathway to understanding, if the paradigm is a good one, or to misunderstanding, if it is not.

Paradigms are always present with us, even if they go unnoticed. The human mind abhors incoherence and demands to fit everything into a single frame of reference, so that it can see how things relate. You, I and everyone else do in fact fit incoming data into categories, which are regularly those of thought and judgment provided by our paradigms, with which we identify – our family, school, club, gang, firm, church or whatever. The paradigms thus operate in our minds like coloured spectacles, or sunglasses, which filter out the glare and cause us to see objects as having a colour that the

glasses themselves have imparted. There is, for instance, a
Marxist paradigm for viewing reality, also a secular humanist
paradigm, and alongside these and others stands the Christian
paradigm. Each paradigm yields a distinctive mind-set and
colours perceptions in a distinctive way, and communication
between the adherents of different paradigms is stultified if
the reality and potency of the paradigms themselves is
overlooked or ignored.

Our present concern is with preaching – preaching viewed
as Christian communication, that is, the communication of
Christianity. The point I want to develop is that in a post-
Christian culture like ours the preacher of the gospel needs
to be aware that the paradigms that currently possess people's
minds rarely match the Christian paradigm that controls his
own thinking. What they take for granted is not identical to
what he takes for granted, nor vice versa. Once, in the
Christendom era, a broadly Christian paradigm could be
assumed in all Western minds, but in today's world that is no
longer the case. So the effective Christian communicator will
be the person who can bring into consciousness and challenge,
in terms of God's revelation, the secular paradigms that
control modern society and the people who make it up. He
needs to understand how these paradigms work, and the best
way to do that is to see where they came from and how they
developed. My point, in other words, is that preachers for
our time need to appreciate the *paradigm shifts* that have
taken place in our culture with regard to God, man and
religion, and to equip themselves for the task of reversing
them.

What is meant by a paradigm shift?
Let me illustrate what I mean by a paradigm shift. Here are
two examples.

The first is the paradigm of the universe, the physical
order of reality to which we belong. Here there have been
several shifts over the centuries. First came the shift from

the earth-centred Ptolemaic world-view, which supposed that the universe consisted of spheres within spheres circling round this planet, to the Copernican heliocentric concept of planets revolving round the sun. Newton then amplified Copernicus by explaining the movements of the planets in terms of universal gravitation, and Einstein amplified Newton by his theory of relativity and curved space. In each era speculative and experimental physicists have fitted their proposed explanations of puzzling phenomena into the currently accepted paradigm.

A second example is the shift from accepting to rejecting external authority as a guide for living, which came about through the European Enlightenment. Starting in England in the 17th century, gathering strength on the continent of Europe in the 18th century, and carrying all before it in the Western world in the 19th and 20th centuries, the Enlightenment was the watershed between the Christendom era and the post-Christian modern world. To characterize it as anti-clerical, as its French exponents did at the time of the Revolution, is not to say enough; at the deepest motivational level, the Enlightenment was an abandoning of all forms of external authority in favour of intellectual and moral individualism. The self-directed, self-affirming individualism that is commonly traced to the Romantic movement rode in on the Enlightenment's back. The effect of this individualism was that one's own personal reason, rather than the church or the community or the cultural tradition, became one's definer of reality; it was for each thinking person to work out for him- or herself a personal solution to the riddles of life. In the 19th century artists and philosophers did this and the guardians of conventional values clucked their tongues, wondering how long it would be before society fell apart. In the 20th century most people have done it, and society today holds together mainly through a shared embrace of materialist values projected by the press and media. For all except conservative Roman Catholics and adherents of some sects, the idea of having one's thought-life and conduct controlled by official church pronouncements, accepted without question because questioning the church is not right, now seems utterly strange and unconvincing. That, we feel, is certainly not the way to go! Nowadays, intellectually and morally, it has to be every man for himself, for no external authority can be trusted fully. Every particular problem must now be dealt with as a matter about which one makes up one's own mind. This modern mind-set evidences a major paradigm shift from the willingness to trust authorities in matters of truth and right that was there before.

This second example of a paradigm shift brings us right up to our present task, which is to focus the post-Christian outlooks in their characteristic form as they relate to the older, Christian understanding of God, man and religion. In this regard, it is possible to generalize about them without being unduly simplistic, even though in terms of positive commitment they fan out, and end up as far away from each other as each is from historic Christianity. But in the terms in which they distance themselves from their Christian heritage they stand pretty much together, and their stance is reinforced by the media, the schools, the world of literature, the news industry and just about every opinion-making institution in North America and Europe, apart from the church itself. And to say 'apart from the church itself' is, alas, something of an overstatement, for significant bodies of opinion within the Christian constituency have themselves accepted attitudes to Christian realities from the drifting post-Christian culture and now seek to define the faith in these terms. Ever since Schleiermacher, the liberal Protestant way has been to keep in step with secular philosophy and adjust Christian belief accordingly, so that it has operated as something of a Trojan horse, or fifth column, in the institutional churches, and many (not all of them Protestants, be it said) are treading this path today.

The result of the shift from Christian trust in external

authority (church or Bible) to post-Christian mistrust of both is, so far as the United States is concerned, rather curious. Americans, as de Toqueville noted long ago, are remarkably religious people, and most of them, it seems, still want to have a Christian veneer on their lives. But when they use Christian words to make Christian-sounding affirmations, it is apparent that many of the words have been redefined and their biblical meaning largely has been forgotten. What is said about God and Christianity in popular religious talk is not what used to be said, and what used to be said (about holiness, self-denial and judgment, for instance) is hardly heard any more. So Christian spokespersons – preachers and teachers, that is – in North America nowadays have to be alert to the problem created for them by the prevalence in their hearers' minds of alien paradigms, just as cross-cultural missionaries have to be. The problem is to ensure that the gospel heard verbally will be understood substantively. That requires both a return to authentic biblical definitions of Christian key words and a corrective interaction with the new paradigms to make room again in people's minds for authentic Christian thoughts. The title of one of Carl Henry's early books, *Remaking the Modern Mind*, aptly sums up the task. One may tackle it by head-on encounter, as Francis Schaeffer did, for instance, or indirectly and in a sense incidentally, as Billy Graham does. But, one way or another, it must be tackled, or our preaching and teaching will achieve little.

We look now at three themes – God, man, and religion, or godliness – to see how at paradigm level minds have changed, and how they need to be changed back again.

God
With regard to God, please note that we stand at the end of four centuries of God-shrinking. In the era of the Reformation the biblical faith in God as one who rules, judges and saves, the source, sustainer and end of all things, took possession

of people's minds in a vivid, clear, compelling way. But by the start of the seventeenth century Lutherans and Arminians were already exalting God's human creatures, and were thus dethroning him at a crucial point. By the end of the seventeenth century, deism, the concept of God as the mighty mechanic who, having made the world, now sits back and watches it go without involving himself in it in any way, was well-established, and thus God was in effect being barred from his world. At the end of the eighteenth century Immanuel Kant, the most influential philosopher for the next one hundred years, silenced God by denying all possibility of God communicating with us in words. Inevitably, therefore, with no word from God to check man's thoughts by, nineteenth-century thinkers equated God with their own feelings and fancies about God, thus absorbing him into themselves in a way that prompted the atheist Feuerbach to comment that when men talked of God they were really talking about themselves in a loud and solemn voice. It was this God, God-in-the-mind as we may call him, whom Nietzsche pronounced dead, and whom Marxists, Darwinists and Freudians decided in due course that they could get on better without.

With that history behind us, it is no wonder that current concepts of God display a drastic diminishing of Reformation faith. Outside conservative Christendom, the man in the street thinks of God in one of two ways. The first concept is of a God who is personal but limited in power, so that he cannot always do what he wants to do or prevent what he would like to prevent. He is prepared to overlook the sins of people who are not in the social sense vicious; he makes no claims, is infinitely kind and tolerant and behaves like Father Christmas, seeking to show benevolence and practise beneficence towards everybody. Process theology draws the profile of this finite, well-meaning, struggling, unipersonal deity. The second concept is of God as an immanent cosmic principle rather than a sovereign person, an animating and energizing aspect of the universe rather than its Maker and its Lord. The latest expression of this concept is found in the New Age movement, in the teaching of people like Shirley MacLaine. It has much in common with the monism of Hindu philosophy, which is known to be one of the main sources of New Age thought.

Neither concept corresponds at all closely to the God of Scripture; each is a misconceived paradigm, needing correction. Here, briefly, is a Bible-based theological grid for the purpose.

The God in whom biblical Christians believe is not a product of human speculation and guesswork, but a self-announcing, self-defining deity who takes the initiative to tell mankind who and what he is. The Bible, which from one standpoint is the interpretative record of God's self-revelation in history, is from another standpoint revelation in its own right, the word of God testifying to himself in the words of men; and in the Bible God shows us four fundamental facts about himself, which we may conveniently alliterate in order to make them memorable.

Firstly, God is *plural*. He is essentially tripersonal, one in three; he is they, a society, Father, Son and Holy Spirit united in a oneness of being that finds expression in an eternal fellowship of love. Jesus, the incarnate Son, reveals by his words and life a relationship between himself and the Father, between the Father and the Spirit, and between the Spirit and himself, in which each seeks honour and glory for the other (see John 14–16). This is the true nature of love, and the ultimate, eternal truth about God's being. God, self-named as Yahweh in the Old Testament, is one in the sense of being the only creator, the only Lord, the only guide of history, the only source of hope for the future; but he is, and always was, triune, though this fact was not revealed until Jesus made it known. Fact it was, however, and it is properly read back into the Old Testament, as indeed the New Testament writers actually do.

The answer given, therefore, to the question *who and what is God?* must be trinitarian. The world's religions and philosophies are ignorant of the trinity; only those who know about the one who made demands of his disciples that God alone has a right to make, who called himself the Son and prayed to one whom he called Father, and who promised, when he left this world, to send one whom he called the Holy Spirit in order to secure a continuance of his presence with his disciples and his ministry to them, know anything about it. The rationalistic and relativized Protestant theology that calls itself liberal has been characteristically unipersonal in its view of God, and has often represented the Trinity as no more than a way of saying that through the God-filled man Jesus we experience God as above us, beside us, and within us, but there is more to it than that. The Father above us, the Son beside us and the Spirit within us are not one person playing three roles (as if God were like the late Peter Sellers, who could play three roles in the same film!), but one God whose nature it is to be three persons in the fullest sense of that word.

Secondly, God is *powerful*. Scripture answers the question, *how does God exist?*, by pointing to the reality of a self-sustaining, self-determining, infinite life that has neither beginning nor end. The mystery of God's *aseity* (derivation of life and energy from himself unendingly) is central to the biblical revelation. All created things are limited one way or another, and sooner or later run out of steam, or decay, but not God! He is like the burning bush, constantly using energy yet remaining just as energetic and potent as before. Created things only continue to exist as he, their creator, actively upholds them in being, but we do not sustain God; God sustains himself.

So Paul, explaining basic theism to the polytheistic Athenians in Acts 17, takes pains to state that God draws life from himself and does not need anything we can give him to keep him going. He gives us life and health and everything that we have; we can give him nothing save our worship. He is not limited by time or space or any power, agency or dimension found in the world that he made. He is omnipotent, omniscient and omnipresent. He is Spirit (that is, personal power and energy, unrestricted). He has life in himself; he is the living God. We cannot direct him, control him or thwart him. He is the sovereign God, the Lord who reigns, God on the throne.

Thirdly, God is *perfect*, in the moral sense of that word. Scripture answers the question, *how does God behave?* by saying, in effect: *gloriously*, from every point of view. Observe the revelation of God's name (that is, his nature and character) in Exodus (it is one of the book's main themes). At the burning bush, the first level of meaning in the name Yahweh is disclosed: it means that God is self-sustaining and self-determining, and makes sovereign covenant commitments (Exod. 3:13-15). Then, after the episode of the golden calf, when Moses, having interceded successfully for the people, says very boldly, 'Now show me your glory' (Exod. 33:18), God allows Moses to see what he mysteriously calls his back and passes before him, proclaiming:

> 'Yahweh, Yahweh, the compassionate and gracious God, slow to anger, abounding in love and faithfulness, maintaining love to thousands, and forgiving wickedness, rebellion and sin. Yet he does not leave the guilty unpunished; he punishes the children and their children for the sin of the fathers to the third and fourth generation' (Exod. 34:6-7).

Here is God declaring his moral glory, his goodness, love, mercy, grace, faithfulness and trustworthiness, patience, forbearance, and readiness to pardon the penitent, alongside his holiness and purity and righteousness, which express themselves in awesome retributive judgment on the impenitent.[2] This is moral majesty, the perfection of a God committed in covenant love, and whose 'name is Jealous'

(Exod. 34:14) – that is, who, like any lover, presses an exclusive claim on the affection and loyalty of the people he loves and blesses. This is the second level of meaning in the name, Yahweh.

Elsewhere, Scripture rounds off its presentation of God as morally perfect by celebrating his wisdom (Rom. 11:33; 16:27; Eph. 3:10). Wisdom means choosing in each situation the best goal at which to aim and the best means for attaining it; God's wisdom means this, as well as man's. The climactic thought about God's moral perfection in the Bible is that all the qualities mentioned – goodness, wisdom, justice – find supreme expression in the redemption of the world through the cross of our Lord Jesus Christ, where heaven's love, heaven's justice and heaven's wisdom met together for our salvation. Blood atonement by penal substitution is looked on askance in some quarters, as if it were an embarrassingly barbaric idea; but the truth is that none of God's doings displays his moral perfection as a covenant God so overwhelmingly. And this leads on to the final point.

Fourthly, God is *praiseworthy*. His works of creation, providence and grace have displayed his glory; now it is for mankind to give him glory in response to this demonstration of his glory. 'Glory' in both Testaments is systematically ambiguous, signifying both God's demonstration of his praiseworthiness and man's responsive offering of the praise that is due. Giving God glory for what we see of his glory will be the life of heaven, and we should be practising for it here on earth. So Paul, a praising man if ever there was one, breaks out repeatedly into doxology in the course of his theological arguments and admonitions (Rom. 1:25; 9:5; 11:33-36; 16:25-27). So the Book of Revelation pictures heaven as a place of praise (chaps. 4, 5, 7, 19:1-10). And the Book of Psalms models glory-giving as the central activity of one's life.

Some have queried the Creator's requirement of worship as if it were dishonourably self-centred. Should a human being make such a requirement, it would be dishonourable and vicious – that we grant. But the Creator is not a human being, and his requirement of us that we focus on him, honour and love him, and show our appreciation of his love for us by praise and adoration is ennobling to our nature; it is entirely appropriate in a love-relationship (yes, the Christian life is meant to be a love affair). And God has so made us that glorifying him is the way of supreme fulfilment for our humanness. When we discover by experience that giving glory and worship to our lover – God – brings supreme joy, delight, happiness and inner contentment, our doubts and hesitations about the divine demand for glory-giving melt away.

Here, then, are the central truths about God of which the post-Christian paradigms – the God who is Father Christmas, and the God who is Shirley MacLaine – lose sight. Our task is to detect and dispel these degenerate and unworthy notions, challenging them wherever they are found, in the churches as well as outside them, and reintroducing those who have been embracing these ideas to the God who is plural, powerful, perfect and praiseworthy in ways that at present they have not begun to conceive. The new paradigm needs correction by the old one; in this case, at any rate, the old is indeed better.

Man

With regard, now, to man, what we face in the modern world is less a coherent paradigm than an incoherent pose, a grandiose self-image produced by wishful thinking that we find impossible to sustain consistently. For the past two centuries, egged on by the Enlightenment, Western man has been playing the role of the Wizard of Oz. We have set up for ourselves a magnificent façade of technological competence and mastery, power and glory, and what could be called our official claim is that man is the measure of all things and the monarch of all he surveys. Behind that façade, however, over the same two centuries, Western man has increasingly found himself unable to avoid feeling that real life is desperately dreadful. Our optimistic triumphalism masks deep pessimism and anxious fear, and we oscillate constantly between the two moods. Politicians, journalists and media people labour to maintain in us the feeling that our society is going somewhere good and that they themselves are helping to lead us there. But writers and artists, who mirror the sensitivities of the culture around them, have long been saying, and with increasing vehemence, that man is not so much the master as the maniac, and that his madness is making for unutterable misery. Dostoevsky and Camus among writers, and Francis Bacon among painters, come to mind as exponents of this theme, who inexorably map modern nihilism and pin-point the guilt, anxiety, loneliness and disgust that it engenders. Publicly, we continue as optimists, talking as if utopia is just round the corner; privately, we have become pessimists, feeling, with Thomas Hobbes, more and more that human life is nasty and with the early Eliot that as individuals we are bankrupt and empty. In our moments of truth we see ourselves as pathetic little persons lurking, Wizard of Oz style, behind our façade of fantastic technology, knowing that our supposed magic is a sham. There is an inward failure of hope, of vision and of nerve. We feel lost – as in truth we are.

What must be said to correct this post-Christian, split-minded perception of ourselves, with its unattainable purpose of re-erecting the broken-down paradigm of man the master? Three things.

First, the human individual's true dignity derives from being made as God's image, steward and partner (Gen. 1:26-28). Exegetically, the basic understanding of God's image in man is to be drawn from Genesis 1:1-25, where God appears as rational, forming and fulfilling purposes; as creative, calling into being what previously did not exist; as managerial, establishing and maintaining order in place of chaos; and as a value-producer, whose achievements are 'very good'. Add to these qualities God's capacity for personal relationships and the moral perfection of his dealings – facets of the divine life already apparent by the end of Genesis 3 – and you have the fulness of the image that man was made to express. Older theology in the Thomist tradition construed the statement that God made man in his own image statically, as if the image consisted in abstract rationality and conscious selfhood as such. But the statement should in fact be understood dynamically, as telling us that God made man upright (Eccles. 7:29), so that he images God more or less according to how far he uses his natural endowments for obedience, love and righteousness, and how far he does not. It is this perspective that explains how Scripture can affirm both the continuance of the image relationship after the fall (Gen. 9:6; 1 Cor. 11:7; James 3:9) and its restoration in Christ by new creation (Eph. 4:23; Col. 3:10). Our human powers as such do indeed image God to some degree, but God-like righteousness is a dimension of the image too, and here it is a matter of less in our natural fallenness and more through the moral transformation that flows from supernatural saving grace (Matt. 12:33; Eph. 2:10). The call to express God's image in our lives remains, however, the basic and universal human vocation.

A further element in human dignity is that as God is eternal and everlasting, so each human being has been created for eternity, and the choices and commitments made in this life have unending significance, since they determine what sort of experience the eternity that follows our leaving this world will be. This world is a vestibule and rehearsal-room for that which is to come, and our doings here will determine our destiny there. (See Rom. 2:6-10; 2 Cor. 5:10). The biblical answer to the feeling that life is trivial and meaningless is that through saving knowledge and steady service of God in Christ we may lay hold of unimaginable glory, whereas failure at this point will result in unimaginable loss. The everlastingness of the individual, and the momentousness of present life as determining future life, are the twin themes to which the Puritan phrase, 'the greatness of the soul', refers, and this destiny-making significance of the present is an aspect of the dignity of man that we need to hear more about from present-day pulpits than we do.

Secondly, each human individual's life has become a *tragedy* – that is, a story of goodness wasted, potential squandered, and value lost. Each of us has fallen from the image of God, and all that is natural to us now is what Scripture calls sin – egocentricity (always looking after number one), pride (always seeking to be on top, in the know and in control), sensuality, exploitation, indifference to evil, carelessness about truth, and a lifelong quest for whatever forms of self-indulgence appeal to us most. Much of this, in our post-Christian culture, is thought of as admirable and ideal, but it all appears vicious and demeaning when measured by the call and law of God and the example of Jesus. It is in fact ruinous folly, and folly of which we are quite unable to shake free by our own resources, for we are by nature slaves of sin. This, the inescapable bad news with which the gospel starts, must be affirmed against all ideas of the natural goodness and perfectibility of man (which ideas are themselves products of egocentric pride).

Thirdly, restoration by grace to life in God's image is the *glory* and *felicity* – the only true glory, and the only lasting felicity – of sinful human beings. Granted, to the self-seeking eye of the natural man the path of faith, love, and obedience, of repentance, conversion, self-denial and cross-bearing does not look like either glory or felicity, but the way of life is in truth to die to self in order to live to God. One loses to gain; one gives up in order to receive; one repudiates and negates the life of self-serving in order to experience new life with Christ in Christ, his resurrection life lived out in and through our own living.

This is the baptismal paradigm: dying to live. In the words of the classic Anglican Prayer Book:

> Remember always that Baptism represents unto us our profession; which is, to follow our Saviour Christ, and to be made like unto him; that as he died and rose again for us, so should we, who are baptized, die from sin, and rise again unto righteousness, continually mortifying all evil desires, and daily increasing in all virtue and godliness of living.

To fulfil this pattern is a life's task; laying hold of God's salvation, which in itself costs nothing, costs everything. Yet those who take this road are rich beyond all telling, for God himself is their shield and their great reward.

The pride, self-sufficiency, proclaimed independence and lurking despair of the post-Christian paradigm of human fulfilment must be challenged antithetically by appeal to the baptismal paradigm of humility, self-denial, acknowledged dependence and happy hope in Christ. Each view of man is a direct negation of the other, and the gospel cannot be grasped where the secular view holds sway.

Religion
With regard to religion, little need be added to what has already been said. The secular assumption is that religion would be seen as a hobby; if practised at all, it will be a venture in self-fulfilment, a quest of a crutch of transcendent help and support. Presentations of Christianity as a recovery of self-esteem (Schuller) or a discovery of health and wealth (Hagin and Copeland) appear to endorse this. But Scripture conceives religion as the living of a life of God-esteem and self-abasement, and of faith in Jesus Christ that blossoms into a love-affair of doxology and devotion, and insists that without such religion life is inescapably maimed. The secular paradigm must be repudiated; the biblical paradigm must be affirmed.

Upside down is the right way up

Ladling Tabasco sauce into a frying pan is not the way to
start preparing a meal, and I do not suggest that orchestrating
a paradigm clash in the pulpit is the way to start preparing a
sermon. But I do suggest that if Christ's messengers fail to
realize how much of the application of sermons will be
filtered out by an alien mind-set in the audience regarding
God, man and religion, they will preach much less effectively
than they might do.

Further, I suggest that preachers who pander to these
secular paradigms and try to fit their message into the frames
that the modern mind-set provides cannot but be unfaithful to
God at a deep level, and put their labour into a bag with
holes. Fragments of truth and wisdom will no doubt get
across, but overall the story of their ministry will be one of
qualified failure due to the distortions involved in their frame
of reference.

So, finally, in preaching and teaching each gospel truth
we should regularly call attention to the difference between
God's viewpoint about himself and ourselves and the
contrasting mind-set of our culture on the same subject. This
task can be looked at picturesquely in the manner of the late
G.K. Chesterton, out of whose book Thomas Howard and I
took a leaf when we titled the last chapter of *Christianity
the True Humanism*, 'Upside-Down is the Right Way Up'.[3]
Through his journalism, apologetics, novels and Father
Brown stories, Chesterton projected a consistent vision of
the human race as intellectually inverted through sin, so that
mankind now naturally lives and thinks upside-down in
relation to the truth that should lead and guide us. It is
commonplace to say that the gospel message, and the Christ
who comes to us in and through that message, turns us upside-
down in relation to what we were before. What is not so
common is to see with Chesterton that to turn upside-down
those who are inverted already is to set them right way up,
and so in a real sense restore them from craziness to sanity.[4]

But that is in fact what the authentic message of Christ will do when set within the authentic paradigms of biblical faith. The pastoral and evangelistic preaching of evangelicals, I believe, desperately needs this emphasis on the proper paradigms in these confused and confusing days, and that is why I have sought to deal with it so strongly and at such length.

Notes

1. Thomas Kuhn, *The Structure of Scientific Revolutions* (Chicago: University of Chicago Press, 2nd ed. 1970), has done more than anyone to give the word technical status, and to focus the idea of a paradigm shift (the replacement of one frame of reference by another, due to some kind of pressure). I make free use of this idea.

2. Punishment for parental sin to the third and fourth generation does not imply the injustice of penalizing innocent parties. There is a back reference to Exodus 20:5, '... punishing the children for the sin of the fathers to the third and fourth generation of those who hate me'. The assumption is that children will follow in their parents' footsteps, and the divine form of words is intended to alert parents to the damage they may do to their families, and to children yet unborn, by sinning, over and above the damage they will do to themselves by provoking God to be angry with them. It remains a stubborn fact that children will do what they see their parents doing.

3. J.I. Packer and Thomas Howard, *Christianity the True Humanism* (Waco: Word, 1985), pp. 231 ff.

4. The title of Alzina Stone Dale's study of Chesterton, *The Outline of Sanity* (Grand Rapids: Eerdmans, 1982), catches this idea, though there is more to it than Dale brings out.

PREACHING HELL
AND
PREACHING HEAVEN

Bruce Milne

4

PREACHING HELL

Bruce Milne

As I approach this topic I do so with a certain amount of diffidence. One of the reasons for this attitude is that this is a topic of great and continuing theological controversy. Whilst my remit is not to address the subjects of heaven and hell but of *preaching* heaven and *preaching* hell, some reference to the debate is inevitable if I am to handle the subject responsibly.

Also, I am diffident for this is an aspect of Christian truth which is, in a quite pervasive sense, foreign to the culture of the Western world. Despite the fact that as a culture we have moved into the post-modern period and in many senses have rejected the instincts and the rational self-confidence of the Enlightenment, our culture remains the child of the Enlightenment, at this point at least, for the notion of eternal personal conscious existence, whether in bliss or torment, is not seriously believed in today. I am referring not only to a mind-set that is out there, for that mind-set is also within the church. All of us need to look at our own convictions, and ask: 'Do I stand regularly gazing across the vistas of eternity? Do I really believe in heaven and hell?'

However, if for these reasons I feel a certain diffidence, I am also aware of a real degree of confidence precisely because of the topics of preaching hell and preaching heaven. It is exactly at this point that the true stature of the Christian preacher emerges. Paul speaks of it in 2 Corinthians 2:14-16:

> But thanks be to God, who always leads us in triumphal procession in Christ and through us spreads everywhere the

fragrance of the knowledge of him. For we are to God the
aroma of Christ among those who are being saved and those
who are perishing. To the one we are the smell of death; to the
other, the fragrance of life. And who is equal to such a task?

The pulpit is erected on the threshold of eternity. What a
privilege, yet what a responsibility. In the words of Thomas
Carlyle, 'Who having been called to be a preacher would
stoop to be a king?'

I will address the topic of preaching hell under three heads:
Why preach hell?; What do we preach when we preach hell?;
How should we preach hell?

Why preach hell?
The simplest and truest answer to this question is, we preach
hell because we have no choice. If we understand our
preaching ministry in terms of the Old Testament prophetic
model then our part is simply to convey what God has spoken.
The call of Jeremiah resonates for all evangelical preachers:
'Then the LORD reached out his hand and touched my mouth
and said to me, "Now, I have put my words in your mouth" '
(Jer. 1:9). So does the call of Ezekiel: ' "Son of man, eat
what is before you, eat this scroll; then go and speak to the
house of Israel." So I ate it, and it tasted as sweet as honey
in my mouth' (Ezek. 3:1, 3). For us as preachers, the scroll
which is delivered to us is the Word of God, the scriptures
of the Old and New Testaments. Our responsibility as
preachers is to tell out that Word, to expound it and to apply
it to all who will hear. To do that faithfully means sharing
the whole counsel of God, both blessings and woes. We
cannot forget the warning of God in Jeremiah 6:14 concerning
the deceitful prophets who 'dress the wound of my people
as though it were not serious. "Peace, peace," they say, when
there is no peace'; or ignore the searching words of Jeremiah
23:16-18:

'Do not listen to what the prophets are prophesying to you;
    they fill you with false hopes.
They speak visions from their own minds,
    not from the mouth of the LORD.
They keep saying to those who despise me,
    "The LORD says: You will have peace."
And to all who follow the stubbornness of their hearts
    they say, "No harm will come to you."
But which of them has stood in the council of the LORD
    to see or to hear his word?
Who has listened and heard his word?'

Our commitment to a biblical, expository, preaching ministry requires that we preach hell as well as heaven, God's awful judgments as well as his unfathomable blessings, his righteous wrath along with his justifying grace. Donald Coggan, in his book *The Sacrament of Preaching*, writes:

> The Christian preacher has a boundary set for him. When he enters the pulpit he is not an entirely free man. He is not at liberty to invent or choose his message. It has been committed to him and it is for him to declare, expound and commend it to his hearers. It is a great thing to be under the magnificent tyranny of the gospel.[1]

If we are faithful expositors of the Bible it is impossible to miss the many passages that describe the reality of hell. We have to clarify what *perishing* means in John 3:16 or what *God's wrath* means in Romans 5:9. Preaching through the Sermon on the Mount we will need to explain 'in danger of the fire of hell' (Matt. 5:22). A series on the parables of Jesus will deal with the weeds which are pulled up and burned in the fire at the harvest at the end of the age (Matt. 13:40), or with the bad fish which at the end will be thrown into the fiery furnace (Matt. 13:50), or the guest without wedding clothes at the heavenly banquet who is tied hand

and foot and thrown outside into the darkness where there will be weeping and gnashing of teeth (Matt. 22:13), or the fate of those on the left hand at the judgment who hear the King pronounce the sentence, 'Depart from me, you who are cursed, into the eternal fire prepared for the devil and his angels' (Matt. 25:41). Luke recounts the parable of Dives and Lazarus with its terrible description of Dives in torment in hell (Luke 16:19-31). Luke also records the words of Jesus: 'Fear him who, after the killing of the body, has power to throw you into hell' (Luke 12:5). Exposition of John's Gospel brings us to deal with 3:36: 'whoever rejects the Son will not see life, for God's wrath remains on him'; or to explain the condemnation which awaits on the last day 'those who have done evil' (5:29). Preaching through Romans requires handling the wrath of God in 1:18. Ephesians 2:3 refers to 'those who were by nature objects of wrath'. An exposition of Philippians brings us to those whose 'destiny is destruction' (3:19). 2 Thessalonians 1:9 refers to 'being punished with everlasting destruction and shut out from the presence of the Lord'. Expounding our way through the Book of Revelation will bring us inevitably to the great white throne from whence those whose names were not found written in the book of life are thrown into the lake of fire (20:1-15). Hence biblical preachers who are faithful to the Lord will inevitably preach hell. The choice is not left to us, it is simply synonymous with faithfulness to our commission.

What do we preach when we preach hell?
This question follows inevitably from the first and it opens up the whole area of biblical and theological understanding. Which theological questions confront us in preaching hell? Let me just mention three.

Firstly, *Is hell real?* Here we touch the question of symbolic language and are concerned with biblical hermeneutics. The English word 'hell' is a translation of the Greek word *gehenna* (for example, Matt. 5:22; Mark 9:43). The term is derived from the Valley of Hinnom, outside Jerusalem, where children were sacrificed by fire in pagan rites (see 2 Kgs. 23:10; 2 Chr. 28:3; Jer. 7:31). In later Jewish writings *gehenna* came to mean the place of punishment for sinners. In the inter-testamental writings, it was depicted as a place of unquenchable fire. The general idea of fire expressing divine judgment is also found in the Old Testament, for example in Deuteronomy 32:22 and Daniel 7:10.

The teaching of the New Testament endorses this belief. Hell is described as the lake of fire (Rev. 19:20; 20:14) and eternal fire (Matt. 25:41). Elsewhere, Jesus described hell as 'outer darkness', a place where there is expressed the most convulsive and bitter regret, weeping and gnashing of teeth (Matt. 8:12, AV). Paul in 2 Thessalonians 1:9 speaks of hell in terms of separation, of being shut out from the presence of the Lord. Hell is a location: the lost go to a place 'prepared for the devil and his angels' (Matt. 25:41).

Some degree of symbolism is surely inevitable, and indeed is indicated by the texts themselves since they speak both of fire and darkness. We are to beware of excessive literalism in interpreting the biblical teaching of eternal punishment. We are moving in a dimension which transcends our terrestrial experience. Symbols, in a sense, are all that we have, but they are unique, God-breathed symbols which do not mislead us. Our part is to hold reverently to them, as to all the revealed words of God. What surely must influence us in taking the biblical language seriously is that the Lord Jesus Christ, on the basis of the symbols that he received from the Old Testament and then himself restated and filled out, expressed the deepest gravity and seriousness with respect to hell.

Secondly, *Will hell be populated?* This question concerns the possibility of universalism. For myself, it is simply not possible to square universalism with the plain teaching of Scripture, for which the passages already cited can serve as sufficient examples. However, the fact that the ultimate salvation of all is so commonly espoused, both within as well as outside the church today, requires that the evangelical preacher be able to demonstrate the inadequacies of the case for universalism, particularly at those points where it is claimed to have some scriptural backing (see John 1:29; 12:32; Rom. 5:18; 1 Cor. 15:28; 1 Tim. 4:10; 1 John 2:2). We need to be ready to show that *in context* these texts do not teach the final salvation of all. Rather, they point to a God who, in his amazing grace, stands ready to receive *all* repentant sinners, no matter their guilt, through the sacrifice and merit of his dear Son, whose atonement is gloriously sufficient and comprehensive enough to save for ever *all* who come to him.

Thirdly, *How long will hell last?* This question concerns the issue of annihilationism. The traditional evangelical position until the very recent period has been to affirm, albeit with a solemn and distracting sense of fear and trembling, the unending duration of the punishment of the impenitent. In the past, annihilationism was confined to the outer fringes of theological reflection. Today, however, this view has made a significant appearance at the heart of evangelical witness, either in the annihilationist form or in the closely related position of conditional immortality. This development has not only created something of a crisis on both sides of the Atlantic as far as evangelical belief is concerned; there is also genuine emotional difficulty among the great company of those who like myself owe an enormous debt both theologically and personally to some of those who have lately, however tentatively, moved in this direction. This is not the place for extended examination of these alternatives. But in my judgment the meaning attached to 'eternal' with respect to the future bliss of the redeemed cannot be transmitted into a reference only to the *result* of judgment rather than a continuation of the *act* of judgment when used of the fate of the impenitent (cf. Matt. 5:22; 18:9; 25:41, 46;

Mark 9:43-48; 2 Thess. 1:7-9; Jude 7, 13; Rev. 14:9-11). In general I find myself in agreement with J. I. Packer's observation that 'its advocates appear to back into it in horrified recoil from the thought of millions in endless distress rather than move into it because the obvious meaning of scripture beckons them'.[2] In my judgment the traditional interpretation is to be upheld, namely the belief in the eternity of the divine judgment in hell. Beyond any question this is a terrible and awesome prospect even for the most depraved. Nor can any of us for a moment forget that 'there, but for the grace of God, go I'. But if we are to be faithful to what God has made known, then within our preaching there needs to be warning concerning the eternal divine retribution.

This brings us to the third of my questions relating to this topic: *how should we preach hell?*

Firstly, *we should preach hell in relation to the character of God.*

Hell is not an arbitrary reality in an independent orbit isolated from the whole body of revealed truth. Rather it is integral to the whole, being in essence the inevitable implication of the revealed nature of God in his confrontation with cosmic evil and sin. In other words it is because God is who he is that there is a hell. Thus our preaching of hell should not strike our congregations as a surprise, as something totally unexpected, out of keeping with all else that they have heard from our lips. In particular it should not appear repugnant to the character of the God on whom we focus in our worship or whose salvation we celebrate in our evangelistic proclamation and witness.

We should preach hell in relation to God at a number of points. First of all, we should preach hell in relation to *his self-revelation*, making it clear thereby that hell is not the product of human speculation or vindictiveness. Hell is not the figment of mean-spirited preachers or warped kill-joys who find perverse delight in the contemplation of their fellow humans experiencing eternal, punitive suffering. The God *who is*, is the God who has spoken concerning himself in the Scriptures. So we believe in and preach hell because God himself speaks concerning it in his Word.

Then, we should preach hell in relation to *the majesty of God*, his sheer Godness, that perfection of the Godhead whereby he is who he is by virtue of his own freedom and glory. We meet him as the one who is exalted infinitely and eternally over us, and therefore the God who is sovereignly free to deal with his creatures in time and eternity as may please him. Isn't that what Jesus was drawing attention to when he spoke of 'fearing the one who can destroy both soul and body in hell'?

We should also preach hell in the context of *the holiness of God*, that perfection of the Godhead whereby he implacably and eternally repudiates all evil. For God, therefore, all evil and sin must be unmasked and exposed and passed judgment upon.

We should preach hell in relation to *the faithfulness of God*, his perfection as the one who is invariably and eternally consistent with himself, the God who remains faithful for ever and who thereby affords stability and consistency to all that is. 'The self-consistency of God, which is primarily one of the comforting and glorious things about him, is a terrible thing in this connection. God does not forget, the injury to the divine order does not heal, this wound remains open eternally. Not in human memory – there it heals only too easily – but in the remembrance of God. The biblical expressions of writing down, entering in a book, and so on, are meant to express this. Just as previously it was comforting to know that we could reckon *on* God, now it strikes terror in the heart to know that we must reckon *with* him.'[3]

We also preach hell in relation to *the justice of God*. The God, into whose hands we fall at death and who summons all his creatures to appear before him in his judgment, is perfectly just in the exercise of his judgment. Hell is the outworking of this perfection, a means of honouring the justice of God.

We should preach hell in relation to *the wrath of God*, his holy and implacable antipathy and resistance to sin and evil.

Thus our persuasiveness in teaching hell will reflect on the consistency with which we have embraced and taught the whole council of God, the full terms of the character of the glorious God as revealed in Scripture.

Secondly, *we should preach hell in relation to our Lord Jesus Christ and in particular his teaching and his atonement.*

As to his teaching, we should make as clear as we can that Jesus Christ believed in *the reality of hell* and warned his hearers regularly concerning it. The one sinless mind in all history, he who had his being in eternity in the bosom of the Father, who told what he had seen in his Father's presence, spoke and taught repeatedly concerning hell. In the words of C. H. Spurgeon:

> You must confess, my dear hearers, that Jesus Christ was the most tender-hearted of men. Never was there one with so sympathetic a disposition. But for all that, not all the prophets put together, though some of them be stern as Elijah, can equal in thundershot the sound of that still voice of him, who albeit he did not cry or lift up his voice in the streets, spoke more of hell and the wrath to come than any that preceded him.[4]

We also should preach hell *in relation to the atoning sacrifice of our Lord Jesus Christ*. There can be no greater manifestation in human history of the holy antipathy of God towards human sin than the cross of Christ. He who did not spare his own Son, by that terrible deed of mercy exposed and revealed for all eternity how terrible is his refusal to ignore or overlook our sin. When we consider all that our

Lord Jesus Christ was subjected to in his humiliation and his sufferings; when we try to sound the unfathomable depths of that cry from the cross, 'My God, my God, why hast thou forsaken me?'; when we stand in awe-filled wonder in Gethsemane and hear the words of Jesus, 'If it be possible, let this cup pass from me', the cup speaking of the wrath of heaven against human sin and evil; then and only then do we begin to get some foreshadowing of hell, of the terrible judgments of God against sin and of God's holy assault upon it.

Thirdly, *we should preach hell in relation to human responsibility.*

Here we wrestle with the issue of human freedom and divine sovereignty. Along with our understanding of God's sovereignty we must have place in our preaching for the responsibility of the creature. In other words, we establish some link between our human action and the judgments of hell. A clear biblical indication of this responsibility is shown by a strand in the scriptures which speak of differing degrees of judgment. Jesus, in Luke 12:47-48, says that there are many blows for those who are more accountable and few blows for those who are less accountable. In Matthew 11:23-24 he contrasts the judgments of Sodom with that of Capernaum and these other cities where he himself had been.

But still we have to grapple with the apparent disproportion between the degree of responsibility on the part of humanity and the degree of the punishment expressed by God in hell. What can we say in that context? Let me state two things that I find helpful.

Obviously we need to stress *the holiness of God.* If one reflects on the one sin of Adam and all the implications of that, we get some sense of what one sin is before God.

Then there is *the depths of his scrutiny.* Every idle word will be required of us. Nothing is hidden, the motives of men will be exposed, says Paul in 1 Corinthians 4:5. He is not presenting God as a sort of heavenly snooper, but rather is conveying a sense of the utter justice of his judgments. It seems to me that where we arrive in the end in facing this question is: shall not the Judge of all the earth do right?

Every mouth will be stopped on that day and the whole world will be held accountable to God (Rom. 3:19). When the judgments of God are finally pronounced there will be no word in challenge; the right of appeal is given but there is nothing to say. This will be the one perfectly just judgment in all of history, and a judgment that all will recognize to be valid, fair and just. On that day, God's mercy will reach as far as divine mercy can possibly reach, we may be sure of that. But, 'it is a dreadful thing to fall into the hands of the living God' says Hebrews 10:31.

Fourthly, *we should preach hell in relation to the balance of Scripture.*

There are two aspects to consider here. First of all, there is the *frequency* with which we deal with this doctrine. To be biblical, in my judgment, means two things. It means not only to believe all that the Bible teaches, but it also means to believe it in the proportions with which the Bible emphasizes and deals with it. A ministry that is repeatedly taking up this subject of hell stands accused of being unfaithful to Scripture perhaps as much as a ministry where the word 'hell' is virtually never referred to. We need the balance of the Scripture.

Secondly, *in relation to the hope of heaven* we need to preach hell. It is instructive that Jesus in his parables of judgment invariably talks about the two destinies: there are two roads, two gates, two foundations, there is the right hand and the left hand. In other words, to preach hell alone is law without gospel and, therefore, pastorally disastrous. The only place where hell is treated without reference to heaven is hell itself. A sermon majoring on hell – and sometimes we may need to stress the judgment – should none the less hold out the hope of heaven, the way of escape, and the riches of

God's grace for all who repent and believe.

There will be a variety of conditions among the hearers. In any listening congregation, although there may be some who need to be challenged in terms of their stubborn refusal to respond to the gospel of grace, there are many others who need a word of hope and mercy and encouragement – and sometimes it is the same person. I can still remember as a student, in a very dark and difficult time in my spiritual pilgrimage, wandering into an evening service in a church in Glasgow. The good man was doing a series on Christian doctrine, and had arrived at hell. The whole sermon from beginning to end was on hell. It was very faithful, but I went out of that church in a deeper darkness than when I came in. There are such struggling souls present every time we preach, so preach hell with biblical balance.

Fifthly, *we must preach hell feelingly.*
On one occasion Robert Murray McCheyne asked his close friend Andrew Bonar on what subject he had preached the previous day. When Bonar replied that he had preached on the wicked being turned into hell, McCheyne asked him if he had preached with tears. That is a valid question and needs to be faced. To be a faithful preacher after the model of our Lord Jesus is not just being concerned with the matter of our preaching but also with the manner of it, what to say and how to say it (John 12:49). Allowance for temperamental difference must be respected, but surely in this area of doctrine there must be the engagement of our hearts.

Being brought up in Dundee, I grew up knowing about McCheyne's great ministry there in the1830s. The story is told of a visitor who came to the church after McCheyne had died and asked the church officer if he would give him a demonstration of how McCheyne preached. So the officer put the man in the pulpit and told him to start to preach, in particular to invite sinners to come to Christ. As the man did so, the officer asked him to start to weep. The man did not do so, for he knew he could not turn that on.

John Stott has some very appropriate words in his book on preaching that we need to take to heart:

> I constantly find myself wishing that we twentieth-century preachers could learn to weep again. But either our tear-springs have dried up or our tear-ducts have become blocked. Everything seems to conspire together to make it impossible for us to cry over lost sinners who throng the broad road which leads to destruction. Some preachers are so pre-occupied with the joyful celebration of salvation that they never think to weep over those who are rejecting it. Others are being deceived over the devil's lie of universalism. Everybody will be saved in the end, they say, and nobody will be lost. Their eyes are dry because they have closed them to the awful reality of eternal death and outer darkness of which both Jesus and his apostles spoke. Yet others are faithful in warning sinners of hell, but do so with a glibness and even a sick pleasure, which are almost more terrible than the blindness of those who ignore or deny its reality.[5]

We need to preach hell feelingly, and quite frankly if we cannot get into that frame I wonder about our right to preach hell at all. We need to plead with people in face of this terrible prospect of judgment.

Sixthly, *we should preach hell with proper reserve.*
We do not consign people to hell and that is an enormous relief. It is God who is the Judge, and so we do not know of any specific case that is a candidate for this terrible judgment, with the exception of Judas. The Puritans had a saying, 'It's a long way from the saddle to the stirrup.' What they meant was this: many in that period died when on horse-back, either by a stroke or heart attack as they were travelling, or by a gunshot wound. But between receiving the shot or the pain and the falling to the ground there was sufficient time for repentance. During my years of pastoral ministry it has been my privilege, a number of times over, to lead people to Jesus

Christ in the last moments of their earthly life, God giving them an openness, a responding grace at the last.

Seventhly, *we should preach hell with reference to the grace of God.*

This surely must be one of our supreme points of application. There is no greater backdrop to the preaching of the good news of Christ, nothing that throws it more clearly into light and joy and fullness than the fact of judgment. Here supremely Jesus stands before us in the greatness of his salvation. He is the One who interposed in his infinite mercy and bore the judgments of heaven against our sin. Here is the supremacy of Christ as a Saviour, that he is able to save us, that his merits atone for the eternity of our judgments. In other words, we are to use the preaching of hell as a platform on which to erect and to display the fullness and richness and greatness and glories of our blessed Lord Jesus Christ and the fullness of his salvation. Let us preach hell in the context of the triumphs of God's grace, as the backdrop to the glories of the salvation of him who died for us.

Finally, *we must preach hell in dependence on the Holy Spirit.*

Karl Barth says wisely concerning Christian preaching that we do not understand what it means until we realize that it is impossible.[6] Here the impossibility confronts us. Who are we to stand before people, holding out the one hope of salvation? Who are we that through our ministries destinies are being determined and heaven and hell being populated? Who is sufficient for this?

God has provided for us in his Holy Spirit. In so far as sinners can be provided for, he is our resource. So the person who preaches hell will be a person of prayer who constantly finds himself on his knees, recognizing his utter helplessness and beseeching God for the gracious help of his Spirit, that in this area as in others he may be found faithful.

References

1. Donald Coggan, *The Sacrament of Preaching*,

2. J.I. Packer, *Crux*, Regent College, Sept. 1990, Vol. XXVI, No. 3, p. 24.

3. E. Brunner, *The Mediator*, Lutterworth, 1942, p. 463.

4. C.H. Spurgeon, Sermons, No. 344, 'Tender Words of Terrible Apprehension', delivered, Nov. 4, 1860 at Exeter Hall, London.

5. John Stott, *Between Two Worlds* (Grand Rapids: Eerdmans, 1982), pp. 276-277.

6. Karl Barth, *Church Dogmatics*, I.2, T&T Clark, 1956, p. 750.

5

PREACHING HEAVEN

Bruce Milne

There is no great pleasure in preaching hell unless it be in
the vindication of God in the display of his justice or as a
foil to the greatness of our Saviour and of his salvation. But
as we turn to consider the preaching of heaven, the grounds
for pleasure abound on every hand.

Yet we have to recognize that, throughout this century,
there has been a widespread diffidence in society about the
whole theme of heaven. As far as I can see, that outlook was
the result of two influential perspectives on society. Freudian
analysis tended to see the whole idea of a heavenly existence
as a sign of weakness, as an inability to face the unpalatable
realities and the unsatisfactory relationships of our lives in
this actual world. Since we cannot handle these, we project
a mythical, idealized world of perfect relationships up in
the heavens. Heaven, therefore, is a kind of crutch to get us
through in the real world. Marxist thought saw the hope of
heaven not so much as weakness, but as wickedness. It was
an attempt to promise 'pie in the sky when we die' and to
obviate the obligation to provide that pie now. Heaven was
part of the bourgeois plot to retain control of the means of
production and, in the process, to keep the proletariat
submissive.

However, in the last decade this dismissal of heaven has
not been so obvious. Post-modernism has promoted a sense
of the limits of the rational and analytical. There is now an
openness to a wider, more wholistic understanding of reality
and the spiritual is once again something worthy of
consideration. Another factor in bringing about this changed

outlook has been the dissemination of reports of near-death experiences. Yet when one has said all that, one cannot make too much of it.

The words of Harry Blamires, written over thirty years ago, still have much validity today. He wrote that 'a prime mark of the Christian mind is that it cultivates the eternal perspective,'[1] that is, it looks beyond this life to another one. It is supernaturally orientated and brings to bear upon earthly considerations the fact of heaven and the fact of hell. In this respect the religious view of life differs fundamentally and comprehensively from the secular view of life.

Why preach heaven?

The answer to this question is very much an echo of our answer in the previous chapter regarding 'Why preach hell?' We preach it because we have no choice, because it is the teaching of God's Word.

In the Old Testament there is only limited certainty at the personal level of personal bliss in the life beyond. True, there are verses such as Psalm 73:24 which says: 'You will guide me with your counsel, and afterward you will take me into glory'; and Daniel 12:2 which says that 'Multitudes who sleep in the dust of the earth will awake: some to everlasting life'. But what is clear in the Old Testament is the corporate vision of the hope of the coming kingdom of God, and at its centre the triumphant ministry of the promised Messiah inaugurating the glories of the new age. At times this kingdom is lyrically depicted: 'The wolf will live with the lamb, the leopard will lie down with the goat' (Isa. 11:6); 'They will beat their swords into ploughshares and their spears into pruning hooks' (Isa. 2:4); 'the earth will be full of the knowledge of the LORD as the waters cover the sea' (Isa. 11:9).

Coming into the New Testament the presence of that promised kingdom is announced. Jesus breaks in with a great proclamation: the kingdom of God is at hand and will shortly be inaugurated, setting up the dialectic at the heart of his message of the kingdom. On the one hand the kingdom has come in him: 'But if I drive out demons by the finger of God, then the kingdom of God has come to you' (Luke 11:20). But over against that, the kingdom is still to come and so we are taught to pray for the coming of that kingdom and to anticipate the glorious inbreaking when the risen Son of man appears on the clouds with power and great glory. In the parabolic teaching of Jesus, this vision and this hope are forced upon us, whether in the declaration of joy of the heavenly marriage feast, or the bliss of the virgins who were found ready, or the guests who were invited from the highways and byways to share the banquet, or the servants who have employed their talents well and receive enhanced new responsibilities, or the people at the King's right hand who receive their inheritance, the kingdom prepared for them since the creation of the world.

Our handling of John's witness will point to the One who promises all who believe in him the gift of eternal life. We hold him forth who is himself the resurrection and the life, who shares his conquest of death with all who believe in him, who has gone to prepare a place for his disciples where one day they will be with him and behold his glory.

Exposition of the opening chapters of Acts requires reference to the Christ who will be sent again at the time appropriate for the restoring of all things (Acts 3:21). In the New Testament letters we stumble against heaven on almost every page, as we with Paul explore the glories of salvation of those who have been called and predestined and glorified (Rom. 8:30), and we join with Peter in praise 'to the God and Father of our Lord Jesus Christ! In his great mercy he has given us new birth into a living hope through the resurrection of Jesus Christ from the dead, and into an inheritance that can never perish, spoil or fade – kept in heaven for you' (1 Pet. 1:3-4). More indirectly, we celebrate the gracious gift of the Holy Spirit who is the foretaste of that coming glory through whom we are 'sealed for the day of redemption' (Eph. 4:30), that day when we shall see Jesus face to face, when we shall be like him (1 John 3:2). The New Testament closes with Revelation 21 and 22 describing the coming of the bridegroom and the descent of the New Jerusalem, the eternal home of the people of God.

Why preach heaven? Because the living God has drawn back the veil in his revelation and permitted some beams of that coming glory to shine upon us, and some echoes of the heavenly music to fall upon our ears and to reach into our hearts, so we cannot keep it to ourselves. We *must* preach heaven.

What should we preach in preaching heaven?
Firstly, we should seek to answer the question, *what is heaven like?* As with hell the question concerns our interpretation of the biblical descriptions, the symbols of Scripture: the holy city and an adorned bride; an idyllic, peaceful and fruitful community; a wedding banquet; a state of overwhelming light and glory; a rapturous choir; a beautiful garden. How are we to interpret all this?

One answer is to take these descriptions *literally,* and that was the answer often given in an earlier generation when, for example, believers spoke about sitting at the gates of heaven. But inevitably we recognize a symbolism in those descriptions of heaven. However, as with hell, the symbols are not arbitrary, they are God-breathed, God-given symbols and therefore we are called to look *through* them as we seek to envision something of that glory which transcends all that eye has seen or ear heard.

Secondly, *how different is heaven from earth?* This question reflects the issue of continuity and discontinuity. Over the years Christian writers and teachers have inclined in both directions. Some are inclined towards a radical discontinuity; heaven is very different from earth, and they appeal to passages such as 2 Peter 3:10-12, which describes the elements being destroyed by fire and the destruction of the heavens, followed by a radical reshaping and remaking. Others, and I would be numbered among them, note the reference 'to a new heaven and a new earth' in 2 Peter 3: 13. The Greek word *kainos*, translated 'new', means 'renewed'.

A pointer towards continuity is the earthliness of the biblical anticipations, which, while necessarily symbolic to a degree, are impressive in their exuberant materiality. Of special significance in this regard is the post-resurrection form of our Lord. In his encounter with the disciples, his material body had not been abandoned: 'Touch me and see,' he said (Luke 24:39), and astonishingly asked, 'Do you have anything to eat?' (Luke 24:41). Surely this points to a new, liberated and radically quickened materiality. Paul in Romans 8:21 writes concerning the liberation of creation from its bondage to decay to share in the glorious freedom of the children of God, a reference that points towards continuity in some sense. Continuity also seems to be called for in the understanding of the indwelling Holy Spirit as the foretaste of heaven (Eph. 1:14).

A final theological argument for continuity concerns the earth as the sphere of salvation. God's conflict with Satan, and humanity's fall under his sway, took place within earthly space and time. Therefore, the vanquishing of Satan and the inbreaking of the kingdom, which will overwhelm and overcome him, ought to take place within our earthly history. The full and final vindication of Christ's conquest as the last Adam ought to have reference to this earth where the first Adam fell. In other words, the work of the Creator can be seen as finally sustained and vindicated in the work of the Redeemer.

Thirdly, we must seek to answer the question, *when will we experience heaven?* This question is concerned with the intermediate state. All who engage in pastoral ministry need to grapple with this because it touches on the way we respond to, and bring encouragement and help and comfort to people, in times of bereavement.

One view asserts that, since to die is to pass wholly out of our human order with its temporal sequence, the dead are immediately removed from temporal consciousness. They fall asleep, using the biblical phrase in its fullest sense, that is, they cease to be conscious. Accordingly, for the dead, the next conscious moment is the *parousia* and the subsequent life of heaven. Heaven is therefore experienced virtually immediately upon death, from *their* perspective.

However, this view is in danger of ignoring a strand of evidence in the Scripture which, while admittedly not expansive, is not insignificant. In 2 Corinthians 5:4 Paul expresses hesitation at the prospect of an unclothed life after death before being clothed again with his heavenly body. His hesitation is an acknowledgment of the abnormality of the intermediate state. Our true goal is the resurrection of the dead, with our resurrection bodies capable of the life of heaven.

But the intermediate life is a validly conscious existence. Moses, who had died 2,000 years previously, appeared on the Mount of Transfiguration with Jesus (Luke 9:30). The promise of Jesus to the condemned criminal regarding his being with Jesus in Paradise also points to a conscious intermediate state (Luke 23:43). Similarly, the story of Dives and Lazarus uses imagery in which an intermediate state is assumed (Luke 16:19-31). Paul comforts the Thessalonians in their concern about deceased loved ones with an assurance that Christ will bring them with him at his coming – this presumes that they are already there with him in the present (1 Thess. 4:13-18). The apostle also states the reality of a conscious experience after death when he writes that to die is to 'depart and be with Christ, which is better by far' (Phil. 1:23). Hebrews 12:23 refers to the spirits of the righteous made perfect as part of the context of Christian worship. The Book of Revelation has a series of visions which depict the saints in worship prior to the end. While arguably duration of time is different for those on the other side of death, still John has the martyrs *waiting* for their ultimate vindication (Rev. 6:10).

Finally, there is the question, *how long will heaven last?* The answer is straightforward: 'we will be with the Lord for ever' (1 Thess. 4:17); 'they will reign for ever and ever' (Rev. 22:5). While the essential meaning of eternal life is no doubt a *quality* of life, yet the quantitative extension was always implicit for Jewish thought – and hence also for Jesus in the absence of clear indications to the contrary in his teaching.

How do we preach heaven?

I acknowledge that today the preaching of heaven is in poor health. It suffers from neglect in many cases and in others it appears regularly to succumb to a certain blandness and unattractiveness, the kind of thing which evokes complaints about the dangers of boredom with endless singing and interminable services of worship. We need to reinstate this great truth to its clear and central position in the Christian consciousness in order to enable God's people to recapture the joyous, radiant anticipation of the early Christian believers as they looked forward to being for ever with the Lord in heaven. How may we do this?

First, *don't over-spiritualize heaven.* In drawing back from a literal interpretation we need to be careful not to become so spiritual that we convey no concept that is clear or attractive regarding heaven.

Secondly, *don't dismiss people's questions about heaven.* In my own church in Vancouver I have been impressed by how many questions I receive about heaven. People grapple with questions such as:

How can I explain death to my children?
Is dying painful?

Is cremation wrong for a Christian?

Is it wrong to grieve when someone dies?

Is it right for a Christian to donate organs for surgical transplant?

Will we know one another after death?

Do the blessed dead in heaven see us now?

What will we do all the time in heaven?

Will we feel sorrow in heaven for those in hell?

Will there be animals in heaven?

What will our heavenly bodies be like and what age will they be?

What about our sexuality in heaven?

What about purgatory?'

These are real questions for many people and pastors need to deal with them. We may not be able to give definitive answers about certain aspects of heaven, but simply to ignore them means that heaven loses reality for our congregations. Somewhere in our ministry we have to find occasion to respond to their questions.

Thirdly, *don't let your doubts about heaven get the upper hand.* Our persuasiveness in preaching heaven will be determined by our personal conviction concerning it. Nothing reduces the effectiveness of our preaching on heaven more than our own struggle or uncertainty about it. There is nothing inappropriate or unworthy about believing wholeheartedly in heaven. Jesus did. It was 'for the joy set before him' that he 'endured the cross' (Heb. 12:2). Jesus lived in the light of heaven, it inspired him, it enabled him to go through the terrors and darkness of Calvary. Let the great biblical passages on heaven sink into our minds. Meditate, pray them over, reflect on them and allow the glorious hope of heaven lay hold afresh, with its wonder and joy, upon our hearts. Reflect on the power of God, recognize his sovereign greatness and majesty, his ability to bring heaven and to establish the age and order of everlasting righteousness.

Recognize the implication of our Lord's resurrection. Christ is the firstfruits of those who have fallen asleep. He has passed through death and will be followed by the teeming ranks of the people of God into the glory and the promise of life beyond the grave. Get these things into our consciousnesses and our hearts as we serve him. So by returning again and again to the Scriptures, prevent your doubts from getting the upper hand.

Preach heaven relevantly
One reason why heaven is not grasped by our listeners nor alive in their hearts is that they do not see the relevance of it. We, in our preaching, need to show them its relevance.

Firstly, *preach heaven as a practical incentive to holiness, evangelism and service.* One great enemy of the biblical preaching of heaven is speculation. Tragically, this area of doctrine has become the happy hunting ground of crystal-ball gazers and apocalyptic dreamers who remove this teaching from the ethical and set it within the purely speculative and at times the farcical. The Bible's teaching on the end times, including its hope of heaven, is always ethical and practical. At the end of 1 Corinthians 15, after his magnificent exposition of resurrection and its implications for the new age, Paul moves to application: 'Therefore, my dear brothers, stand firm. Let nothing move you. Always give yourselves fully to the work of the Lord, because you know that your labour in the Lord is not in vain.' In 2 Peter 3:11, Peter follows his description of the apocalyptic conclusion to history with the challenge, 'What kind of people ought you to be?' When the Bible shares the hope of heaven we need to work it through into its practical applications. I will briefly mention five of its aspects.

(1) Heaven proclaims the impermanence of earth. It is a call to set our hearts on the things above, a call to a true spirituality and unworldliness of heart, a call to have

treasures in heaven which are utterly secure.

(2) Heaven confronts us with our future. And what a future
it is! It is a future of righteousness, of holiness. Therefore,
preaching heaven is a summons to be conformed to the
righteousness of the kingdom in the present, in anticipation
of all that will come in the future.

(3) Preaching heaven is an incentive to evangelism, in
view of the triumph of God's purposes and the greatness of
his salvation. We are renewed in our concern to take pains
to spread the good news of Christ, to beseech lost people to
turn to the Saviour and to receive among all his many gifts
the promise of heaven.

(4) Preaching heaven will remind our people to respect
and preserve the natural environment which will share in
the coming renewal of the new heavens and new earth.

(5) Preaching heaven will help our people to serve their
neighbours lovingly within this present society, struggling in
its fallen order to represent the values of the kingdom of
God – the values of peace, justice, equality, tolerance,
sympathy, a concern for the vulnerable and the weak. The
values which heaven proclaims will endure despite all the
indications to the contrary. Right will triumph.

The assurance of the life of heaven is far from promoting
our lassitude and a quietest withdrawal from the demands
and ministries of the kingdom. Heaven should be preached
as a major incentive to service, to build up the church, to
promote its readiness as a chaste and spotless bride ready
for the embrace of its heavenly bridegroom and the wedded
bliss of heaven.

Secondly, *preach heaven as the assured future of every child
of God.* One of the reasons for lack of joyful anticipation of
heaven is simply the lack of assurance of salvation in so
many of our people. So many of our church members lack
certainty as to this reality and if you doubt that, ask this
question of your congregation: 'If you were to die tonight

and appear before God, what reason would you give for God to let you into his heaven?' Start with your leaders and you *may well* be astonished. Many Christians look to their Christian lives and service for their hope of heaven and their justification before God.

We need again and again to open up the glories of the doctrine of justification: 'being justified by faith we have peace with God through our Lord Jesus Christ and therefore we glory in anticipation of heaven, the hope of glory that is to come' (Rom. 5:1-2). In justification the full righteousness of Christ is credited to believers, and it is their token to a place in that righteous eternity. There is no condemnation to those who are in Christ Jesus, and they should be rejoicing in the hope of the glory of God. We need to clarify to our people that, having been called and foreknown and justified by God, they should have the assurance of heaven.

One of the great statements in Scripture of the assurance of the people of God with respect to the hope of heaven is Revelation 7:9-17. What does John see in that vision in Revelation 7? Here is a great company in the presence of God, drawn from every tribe and people and language and tongue, celebrating his salvation. Now, what company is that? This is a company that John has never seen before. He has a vision of the whole company of the people of God in their celebration of the praises of God. In that company of the redeemed from all the ages gathered in the presence of God in glory, John saw you and saw me. That is how certain it is. We have already been seen in heaven. Hallelujah! What a basis for assurance.

Thirdly, *preach heaven as the recognition of faithful service.* This is an element of the Bible's teaching about heaven from which we instinctively recoil. The whole notion of our service being recognized appears contradictory to the grace of God by which alone we are saved. It even appears a repugnant notion, since it seems to detract from God's sole glory.

However, whatever our hesitations, Scripture speaks of heavenly rewards without embarrassment. In Matthew 5:12, the persecuted are reassured with the promise that great is their reward in heaven. Ministry to Christ's servants, even the smallest act like giving a cup of cold water, will not lose its reward (Mark 9:41). John in Revelation 11:18 speaks of the climax of history as the time for the dead to be judged and God's servants rewarded. Paul is in the same vein in 1 Corinthians 3:8 where he writes that if a man's work passes the test he will receive a reward.

We cannot eliminate this element. Rabbi Duncan famously said: 'If there is anything in which I might be prone to contradict my Lord, it would be if he were to say to me, Well done, good and faithful servant.' We understand that sentiment, but we must remember that Scripture does not speak in that way. John Calvin made the helpful observation that here we are dealing not with servants' wages but with sons' and daughters' inheritances.

Richard Baxter chides believers for their hesitation along this line. He speaks of these acts of service and ministry that we do as Christ's work in us. He encourages us to take them seriously for, in attempting to give all honour to the Christ outside us, we may be forgetting the Christ within us. This is what he wrote: 'While we deny this inward sanctifying work of his Spirit and extol free justification, which are equal fruits of his merit, we make him an imperfect Saviour.'[2] We must affirm the reality of Christ in us and that will include recognizing that rewards in heaven are an affirmation of that. Therefore, preach heaven positively as the recognition of faithful service.

Fourthly, *we preach heaven as the coming victory of right over wrong.* In the Old Testament's anticipations of the kingdom there is a strong emphasis on the righteousness of that coming order. Passages such as Isaiah 11 and Psalm 72 speak of the Messianic King who will reign in righteousness and take pity on the weak and the needy. This sense of the righteousness of the coming order is enormously important, for so many grapple with the deep, dark enigmas of history and of experience: the strange absence of God in desperate circumstances; the mysterious virulence of evil in a world where Christ has lived and died and risen again; the tragedies that break into human life and love and experience.

It is part of our pastoral ministry to struggle with our people through these things and to minister to them in the midst of them. For behind it all there is a great longing for justice, for the victory of right over wrong. Preaching heaven is the proclamation of the end of the ambiguities, the unveiling of the enigmas, the everlasting triumph of justice and goodness and truth. In other words heaven is a world of hope and we are to teach our people to live hopefully in the assurance of the coming triumph of God.

Fifthly, *preach heaven as the defeat of sin and death.* This aspect follows from the last point, but it is more personal. Sin and death are the twin ogres that haunt our race and threaten us all. Life here is lived in an unending battle with temptation, sin and evil and under the ever-lengthening shadow of our inevitable end.

In every listening congregation these tyrants are exercising their sway. But heaven is the great good news that the tyrants have fallen and are mortally wounded, that sin's guilt can be pardoned, that evil's power can be broken, that death's sting can be drawn. Heaven is the certain future in which sin is removed and death is no more.

Sixthly, *preach heaven as the glorification of our Lord Jesus Christ.* In Revelation 5 there is the magnificent vision of the Ancient of Days upon the throne, celebrated by all the myriad hosts of heaven. Then suddenly the focus is upon the wounded Lamb who moves to the throne at the centre of the vision. When he joins the Ancient of Days upon the throne,

the whole host of heaven cries out, 'Worthy is the Lamb.'
Jesus will see the travail of his soul and be satisfied. Now
he is vindicated and raised up and exalted and glorified.
The Lamb is the lamp of heaven (Rev. 21:23), the
illumination of the people of God in heaven is the resplendent
glories of Christ.

Finally, *preach heaven as our fulfilment in God.* This is
what Richard Baxter called 'our fruition of God',[3] that is,
our enjoyment of God, our fulfilment in God. Surely nothing
makes heaven more attractive and more desirable, whether
to ourselves or to our congregations, than the recognition
that it represents the supreme realization of our knowledge
of and our communion with the living God, our Creator,
Redeemer and Sanctifier.

Heaven, whether expressed in more direct worship or
the worship of undreamed of forms of ministry in service,
represents an ever-deeper exploration of and ever-closer
communion with that gloriously indescribable, supremely
attractive, overwhelmingly adorable Being who is our
glorious and gracious God – Father, Son and Spirit – whom
we now know in part but whom then we will know even as
now we are known by him. Oh think of it, to draw near to
God.

To behold, in his majesty, the everlasting Father; to
consider the greatness and vastness of his wisdom in the
infinite extent of his purposes, to see him in his holiness and
righteousness, in his mercy and grace, in his sovereignty and
beauty.

To draw near to his dear Son our Saviour, our great
prophet, the truth incarnate; and now made known, in all his
depth and richness, as our priest in sacrifice; in sympathy
entering afresh into his heart, telling and re-telling the wonders
of his salvation; our King reigning over us, as we endlessly
celebrate our lives for him; to see him in his glory, seeing
him face to face, and feeling upon our hearts evermore the

reality of his personal love for us and for all his people.

To do this in the context of the whole people of God, in all their richness and fullness, from all the ages and from all the areas and from all the cultures of the world, to be united together in the presence of God, and to spend the ages as they unfold in an ever-deeper appreciation and communion and depth of relationship with this great, glorious and indescribably wonderful God.

For this, my dear sisters and brothers, we were created. For this we were made. And heaven is its realization.

Notes
1. Harry Blamires, *The Christian Mind*, SPCK, 1963, p.67.
2. Richard Baxter, *The Saints Everlasting Rest*, London, n.d., p. 33. An edition of this book is published by Christian Focus.
3. Ibid, p. 10.

PREACHING FROM
THE OLD TESTAMENT

Alec Motyer

6

PREACHING FROM
THE OLD TESTAMENT

Alec Motyer

It is interesting to speculate how the Lord Jesus Christ would
have replied had he been asked, 'Why do you keep quoting
from the Old Testament?' It is most likely that he would
have said 'The Old what?' And if we had pressed on with
our question he would in the end have replied, 'Oh, I see,
you mean the Scriptures, the Word of God. Why call it by
such an odd name?'

In this sense there is no such thing as 'the Old Testament'.
Therefore, in asking me to speak about *preaching from the
Old Testament* you have given me a non-subject. If you ask,
'How does one preach from the Old Testament?', the answer
is, 'How does one preach from the New Testament?' There
is no special mystique or approach to preaching that has to
descend on preachers when the Lord leads them to minister
from the Old rather than from the New. There are no special
avenues into preaching from the Old Testament nor any
special tricks of the trade that I can share with you.

But in order to prove my point, let me compare preparing
a sermon from a New Testament passage with preparing a
sermon from an Old Testament passage. The New Testament
passage is Mark 14 and 15. These chapters describe how
the Lord Jesus was brought first of all to the high priest, then
to Pilate, then to the praetorium and then to the cross. If I
wanted to preach on that passage, my basic theme would be
the journey of Jesus step by step to Calvary. I then would ask
what is the central truth in each section, and so my sermon

would begin to emerge from the very structure of the scripture itself.

The Old Testament passage is Exodus 19. In this chapter is told the story of the three ascents of Moses to the top of Mount Sinai. One ascent occurred immediately when he arrived there (verse 3). The second took place after he had come down and called for the elders and set before them the words of the Lord. When he had heard their response he went back up. The Lord gave him further briefing and sent him back down again (verses 7-8). The third ascent is described in verse 20: 'The LORD came down upon the top of Mount Sinai and called Moses to the top of the mount.' It is exactly the same exercise that we found in Mark 14 and 15; we have not invented the division, it is the way that the story is told.

Having divided the passage we are now in a position to preach from Exodus 19. The next question to ask is, What is the chapter about? I think the chapter is about how God's people meet with him. Plainly, it is a story of three interviews with the Lord at Mount Sinai. And there is a different central idea attached to each of the three ascents. The central idea in ascent number one is the idea of *redemption* – the Lord's people meet with God on the grounds of redemption from Egypt (verse 4). The central theme of the second ascent is the theme of *revelation* – the Lord sets up a system of revelation, with Moses as the person who is going to mediate the word of God to Israel (verse 9). The theme of the third ascent is *sanctification* (verses 21 and 22).

But the point I am making is that there is no difference between preparing to preach from Exodus 19 and Mark 14 and 15. Therefore, I would say that there is no such distinct discipline called 'Preaching from the Old Testament'.

Difficulty in preaching from the Old Testament is not inherent in the Old Testament itself. Rather, it is something to do with the way in which we think about the Old Testament. We see it as a book which has attached to it special problems which do not belong to the New Testament. Therefore, we think that there must be a special technique for handling such a strange piece of literature.

I will discuss four reasons why preaching from the Old Testament is often regarded as difficult.

First of all, we hesitate in approaching the Old Testament because we *are troubled by Old Testament criticism.*

When I first heard specialist lectures on the Old Testament during my years at university, the burden of those lectures was that the Old Testament is not what it seems. For example, I was informed that Amos was the first monotheist, therefore if I wanted to understand the Old Testament I was not to start at the beginning with Genesis but with Amos. According to my lecturers Genesis 1 was actually written very late, in the post-exilic period. They also confidently declared that Genesis 1 and Genesis 2 contradict each other. What I had blandly assumed came from the pen of Moses I now was taught came from the pen of at least four other authors. Where I had read Isaiah happily as though it were one author, I was informed that at least three people were involved.

Now these things are not negligible. Even though we are persuaded that it may be otherwise, they build up in our minds a sense that we are dealing with literature which has to be handled with kid gloves. We are hesitant to put our foot into a book about which there are such differences of opinion. But we are called by God to handle the Bible as we have it. And the Bible as we have it is the Bible that Jesus validated. We have to be resolute, therefore, in our handling of the Old Testament.

Preaching from the Pentateuch

I was once asked to address a Christian Union on the subject of the Pentateuch. It really is a massive subject and, absurdly, I was only given fifty minutes for my lecture. It was, therefore, something of a biblical challenge – but, on the other hand, if the Pentateuch could be seen as a whole, with a coherent structure, then its message would automatically emerge.

At a glance it is evident that the Pentateuch falls into two unequal parts. Genesis 1–11 gives the impression of an increasingly crowded world and deals with great universal and cosmic events: Creation, the Fall, the Flood and the Scattering at Babel. But, stepping in to Genesis 12, there does not seem to be anyone about except Abram! And even though Abram's family does increase after a slow start and becomes twelve tribes, the narrow focus of attention remains.

Looking forward from Genesis 12, we can see two 'mountain peaks', in chapters 15 and 17. They are the high points in the Lord's dealing with Abram (who became Abraham in Genesis 17). Genesis 15 is God coming in covenant grace to pledge his promises to Abraham, and Genesis 17 is God coming to put his covenant into practice, but declaring to Abraham in the process the patriarchal law, 'Walk before me and be perfect.' In short, grace and law.

When we come to the Book of Exodus we find that there are also two peaks or high points of God's dealings with his people: one is Exodus 12 and the other is Exodus 20. The Lord said that he would not only bring the Israelites out of Egypt, but that he would bring them to himself. Bringing his people to himself is the explanation of the Passover, which again for convenience we will call grace. It's the grace of the redeemer-God coming down to make his people to be at peace with him. But having introduced them to his grace in the blood of the lamb, what does he immediately do with them? Bring them into the land of Canaan? No. He leads them to Mount Sinai. The Lord's first concern with his covenant people was to tell them his Law so that they may know how to live so as to delight him. They were not given the Law in order to become his people but because they were his people. Again we see grace and law are wedded together in an eternal wedlock. And the Pentateuch begins to make sense.

Grace is spelled out in the Book of Leviticus. In Exodus

25–40 we are given the details of the tabernacle where God, in grace, lives amongst a people who have been saved by the blood of the lamb. The tabernacle is the climax of redemption (Exod. 29:42-46), and the tabernacling of God is spelled out in the Book of Leviticus. The passover sacrifice is amplified into the Levitical system. And the obedience required by God (Exod. 19–24) is amplified in the Book of Deuteronomy as the authorised elaboration and application of the law of Sinai.

At this point the Pentateuch began to look like this:

Genesis 1-11		Genesis 12–Deuteronomy 34				
Universal	Gen. 15	Gen. 17	Ex. 12	Ex. 20	Lev.	Deut.
Backdrop	Grace	Law	Grace	Law	Grace	Law

But what is the Book of Numbers about? It is about the forty years in the wilderness. But it is the oddest piece of history that we will ever read, for the author only describes three things that happened! That is the way the Bible writes, indeed it is in principle the way every historian essentially writes history, for every historian is a selector. All history has to be selective; even those historians who say that history is just one event after another, have to select what they think is important. The only difference between Bible history and what is rather grandly called western scientific history is that the Bible thinks that God is important whereas western scientific history thinks that kings and prime ministers are important. What is called history today is politically or socially orientated, but Bible history is religiously orientated. But all history is selective, and the Book of Numbers is selective.

It would be lovely to go through the three incidents that are recorded, but the details concerning Balaam will do as an illustration. Balaam is represented as a head-on challenge to the Abrahamic promise. He was brought by Balak to curse the Israelites, but the Lord turns the curse into a blessing. The theme of the Book of Numbers is that when the Lord

brings people into covenant with himself he is the guardian
of their covenant reality. The message of the Balaam story is
that the Lord throws a secret net of protection around his
covenant people, in other words, covenant care.

The structure of the Pentateuch is now coming into focus
as a whole.

Gen 11	Gen 12-14	Gen 15-17	Gen 18-Ex 11	Ex 12	Ex 13-18	Ex 19-25	Ex25-Lev	Num	Deut
Universal	Care	Grace and	Care	Grace	Care	Law	Grace	Care	Law
Backdrop		Law					elaborated		elaborated

The Pentateuch is thus throughout a covenantal document,
structured to reveal different facets of covenantal life. The
'grace' sections explain the spiritual and religious basis of
the covenant; the 'law' sections open up the moral implications of the covenant; and the 'care' sections lay a foundation
by revealing the divine will pervading the covenant, the
determination of the Lord to take, make and keep a people
for himself. Likewise, 'covenant' links the universal
backdrop with the particularised history of Abraham and his
covenant family, for the covenant idea is first introduced in
the history of Noah and thus, via Genesis 12:1-3, becomes
the mode in which 'all nations will enter into their
blessedness' in Abraham's seed.

Could you preach on the Pentateuch next Sunday? Of
course you could.

Preaching from Judges
Have you ever asked yourself why the Book of Judges was
written: the author of the Book of Judges, like any other author,
had an objective that he wanted to fulfil. The first sixteen
chapters of his book is a most colourful collection of
characters, with their marvellous exploits and their sometimes
attractive and sometimes dismaying characters. But when
we read Judges 17 it is like going out of the sunlight into a
dark cellar: dark and dismal, indeed even dank and

unwholesome. We meet a Levite who has a concubine; we read of the men of Gibeah burning with lust to have homosexual relationships with the Levite, but instead the poor concubine is turned out to them and they abuse her all night, so that by morning she is dead. What an extraordinary story! Suddenly we have come down from the glittering heights of the Judges and their exploits to where ordinary people live, and we find that underneath the brilliant exterior there is absolute rottenness in the people of God – religious apostasy, immorality, social unrest. Then we look back at the figures of the Judges and we find the recurring comment: 'the land had rest for a certain number of years', and we realise that these great figures are written up as great failures. The author, looking back on this period of history, saw people with brilliant capacity who achieved nothing for the people of God except a temporary passing relief. Their mighty failure was that they did not keep the people of God loyal in their worship or pure in their lives or united in their society.

The author of Judges, however, has a solution to offer – and this is the purpose of his book. The recurring refrain found in Judges 17:6; 18:1; 19:1 and 21:25 says it all: If only there was a king...! The Book of Judges lays the Messianic foundation for the rest of the Old Testament and begins the hunt for the true and perfect King who is depicted, for example, in Isaiah 9 and 11 and fulfilled in our Lord Jesus.

Now in these two exercises in Bible Analysis I have not done any thing other than what we are all accustomed to doing with the New Testament. It is just a matter of taking the Bible seriously as it stands. The structure is the message.

A second line of difficulty as we approach the Old Testament is that *we have lost our sense of the unity of the Bible*. The chairman referred to my animosity against the blank page between Malachi and Matthew. Malachi in his last chapter predicted the forerunner of Jesus, and Matthew says that he has come. Why do they need a blank page between them?

But to help you get my point, regarding the unity of the
Bible, I will ask this question: Who is the New Testament
about? It is about the family of Abraham, for Christians are
the children of Abraham by faith in Christ Jesus. Paul says
in Philippians 3:3 that New Testament believers are *the
circumcision*, by which he means they are the *only* circumcision. It seems to me, therefore, that there is no break from
the point of view of people between the Old Testament and
the New, the family of Abraham are still the family of Abraham,
the Israel of God is still the Israel of God. The term, the
New Israel, never occurs in the Bible because there cannot
be such a thing; there is only one Israel, one chosen people.

It is very important for us to have that perspective. To my
way of thinking, it is very unfortunate that the translators of
our English Bible import the word 'Jew' into the translation
where the Hebrew says a 'Judean' or a 'Judahite', that is to
say, a person belonging to the political province of Judah.
Judaism, from which the term 'Jew' comes, is an inter-
testamental development which is only tangentially related
to the Old Testament. It is a plant which the heavenly Father
of Jesus did not plant (Matt. 15:13). The Bible tells the story
of one God and of one family.

Appreciating the unity of the Bible will disabuse us of so
many mental blockages to preaching the Old Testament. But
there are certain ways in which this first and larger portion
of the Word of God can help us.

First of all, it is the *genuine preparation* for much of the
contents of the New Testament. For example, the best
background to Baptism and the Lord's Supper is the acted
oracles of the prophets in the Old Testament. Jeremiah 19 is
a striking example of an acted oracle, where he wanted to
communicate to the Jerusalemites and their leaders that the
Lord was planning to scatter this sinful and unrepentant
community in such a way that it could never be reconstituted
in their present form. So he took an earthen vessel and went

down to a place called the Potsherd Gate. I suppose it was called the Potsherd Gate because that was where the potters of Jerusalem dumped their unsaleable commodities, and the place would be littered with broken pots and chippings and all manner of discarded utensils. There Jeremiah preached his message of scattering, and at the climax of the message he took the earthen pot that was in his hand and dashed it down amongst all the scattered pieces of earthenware. It was a magnificent picture that the community was about to be fragmented and could never be reconstituted. Who could possibly bring it together again?

But his actions were more that just a visual aid. His acted oracle actually embodied the Word of God. When the prophet enhanced his spoken message with a visual message he was giving the Word of God double effectiveness. The acted oracle lets the Word of God out into the situation in a new and vigorous fashion. He was not just communicating with their minds in a vivid way, he was expressing the Word of God with double force.

Cannot you use that the next time that you preach about Baptism or the Lord's Supper? Is there a better way of understanding the Supper of the Lord than that the bread and wine are an acted oracle and that here the Word of God is concentrated, coming to me for my reception? The very Christ word coming to me vividly expressed, the Word embodied for my reception, the Word of God in all its power and reality.

Rightly at Easter time we preach about the Passover because it is God's own visual aid, in the modern sense of that term, concerning the Cross of our Lord Jesus Christ. In preaching on the Passover, I often use this outline: (1) God is *satisfied* because he saw the blood of the lamb (Exod. 12:13); (2) God's people are *safe* because the destroying angel cannot touch them (Exod. 12:23); (3) the blood is the death of the *substitute*, a perfect lamb, who exactly matched the number and the needs of the people of God (Exod. 12:4). Have I done anything unusual with that story? Although it is

in the Old Testament, would you not preach a New Testament
story in exactly the same way?

So Old Testament prepares us for the New. But the Old
Testament also *supplements* the New. I think the main way
in which the Old Testament supplements the New concerns
the doctrine of creation. It would be hard to preach about
creation if we only had the New Testament in our hands. The
Old Testament declares to us a fourfold perspective on the
creation. We tend to think of creation as how everything
began, but that is only a quarter of the Old Testament doctrine
of creation. What else does it tell us? Not only is God the
originator of creation (Gen. 1:1–2:3), he is also the one who
maintains everything in existence (Isa. 42:5). If for a split
second he forgot, there wouldn't even be nothing, he
maintains everything in existence. Furthermore, he controls
everything in its operation (Isa. 40:26; 54:16-17) and he
guides everything to its appointed destiny (Isa. 65:17-18).

Here is another way in which the Old Testament casts its
own light by way of revelation upon situations in the New
Testament. In the opening verses of Psalm 51 there are three
words for sin, three words which express God's attitude to
the sinner, and three words which say what he can do about
sin – nine key words in three verses.

What is sin? The three words are 'transgressions',
'iniquity' and 'sin'. Sin is the specific thing, iniquity is the
rottenness in our heart from which it flows, and transgression
is the wilful rebellion against God that makes me a sinner.

The three words which speak of God's attitude to the
sinner are 'mercy', 'unfailing love', and 'compassion'.
'Mercy' or 'favour' is the Old Testament equivalent to the
New Testament word 'grace', with exactly the same
significance of unmerited, undeserved kindness freely given.
Its first appearance in Genesis 6:8 says it all. 'Unfailing
love' is love arising out of a determination and commitment
of the will. It is the love expressed in the 'for better, for
worse' undertakings in marriage; it is above the fluctuations

of feeling, a constant 'ever-unfailing' devotion (Jer. 31:3). By contrast 'compassion' is surging, emotional love (1 Kgs. 3:26), the love of 'being in love'.

The three things that he can do with sin are 'blot out', 'wash' and 'cleanse'. Each one of those words has its own message and flavour. The first points to sin as a mark or stain which God can see – and can remove (Num. 5:23; 2 Kgs. 21:13); the second is a launderer's verb, the application of such a detergent as can remove even the most ingrained dirt (Ex. 19:10; Lev. 13:6; Mal. 3:2); and the third is a verb primarily used in Leviticus: sin erects a barrier to fellowship with God and this barrier must be broken down (Lev. 11:32; 12:7). The point of this probing into Psalm 51 is to show that the Old Testament, like the New, has its great theological words and that in the case of the Old, just as in the New, Bible words have Bible meanings.

A third feature of the Old Testament which I believe does make us slightly hesitant about coming to it freely as the Word of God in our preaching *is the existence of moral problems in the Old Testament.* This is a subject in its own right and all I can do is take an instance here and there.

Many lament the element of savagery in the Old Testament. It seems to me, to be frank with you, to be a piece of double think because I don't suppose that there ever was such a savage or unfeeling society as that in which we live. But they take leave to object to savagery when it comes in a book that purports to be the Word of God. Nevertheless the present state of society gives us one perspective from which to approach this sense of disquiet. As a society we have lost our sense of *moral outrage.* The dreadful history of the world over the last forty years has atrophied our sense of moral appreciation of things and, therefore of all societies that have ever been, we are less in a position to pass a judgment on those aspects of the Old Testament which often come under the heading of moral problems.

There are two comments I want to make. First of all, the Old Testament is *full of realism*, and many of the so-called moral problems of the Old Testament are simply due to the spirit of realism that animates the entire Bible. It tells us how things are, that the world is a warlike savage place, and if the Old Testament contains more of this material than the New Testament, the explanation is that it is a longer book.

Psalm 137

One example of this realism is a verse which I think very often troubles the hearts of those who want to adopt an attitude of devout reverence and acceptance towards the Old Testament as the Word of God. The verses are Psalm 137:8-9: 'Happy shall he be... that taketh and dasheth thy little ones against the rock.' How can that possibly be the Word of God?

Psalm 137 is one of the imprecatory Psalms, a feature of which is the ferocity of the psalmists' attitudes to people who have offended. At the same time these writers reveal a spirituality that we would covet. In this Psalm we cannot read it without feeling that the people described were marked by the longing for the things of God. Nevertheless they did come to this rather troublesome conclusion in verse 9.

I suggest to you that the answer lies in the word that is translated 'blessed' or 'happy'. It is the Hebrew word 'ashrey' and if you consult Mr Young and Mr Strong, those perpetual friends of the Bible student, you will find that this word has three uses in the Old Testament, and in any given context you have got to decide which one is appropriate. The first use means 'blessed', under the blessing of God (Ps. 32:1); the second use means 'fulfilled within one's own nature', living a full and happy life (Ps. 1:1); neither of those meanings will fit the context. The third meaning is 'doing that which is morally justified', moving along the right moral course (Ps. 106:3; Prov. 14:21). This is the meaning of the verse and it is technically called the *lex talionis*, or the law of an eye for an eye. In other words, the punishment fits the crime.

Our society has abandoned as savagery the idea of an eye for an eye and a tooth for a tooth. I want to say to you, God help the society that abandons an eye for an eye and a tooth for a tooth, because it is the law of equity that the punishment must exactly match the crime. And the implication of Psalm 137 is that the *lex talionis* is the way that God runs the world.

Elisha and the female bears

Another example that troubles people is the incident involving Elisha and the female bears (2 Kgs. 2:23-24). It is often assumed that what we have here is a cantankerous old man with a bad-tempered God who uses the two bears to kill forty-two innocent children. But Elisha was not an old man, he was a young man who had just taken over from Elijah. Bethel was a centre of idolatry where Jeroboam set up his alternative place of worship. The word which the NIV translates as 'youths' (v. 23) is used in Genesis 37:2 of Joseph at the age of seventeen; 'youths' in verse 24 is a different word which occurs, for example, in 1 Kings 12:8, 10, 14 of the contemporaries of Rehoboam who was aged about forty-one. Even the more exact understanding of the words begin to paint a different picture.

The situation was a critical one: Elisha, the new prophet, faced and was faced by the old, established, apostate priesthood at Bethel. For each party, the future was at stake. The priests could make no headway against Elijah, but perhaps they could put the new man in his place before he grew into his new role. Consequently they arranged a reception committee of 'young louts' to show the inexperienced prophet who was master in Israel. It is not, therefore, a case of a crabbed old man cursing tiny children, it is a case of the new youthful prophet being challenged by the old idolatry. So what does Elisha do? Since it was a spiritual challenge, he met it in a spiritual fashion. He made it a matter of prayer, he cursed them in the name of the Lord. And the Lord, to the praise and glory of his name, stood by his beleaguered servant and sent the two bears.

Are you beginning to feel that you could preach about Elisha and the she-bears? Do you want a God who stands by his people or not? Of course, if you don't want that sort of God, then this story is not saying anything to you. But if you feel the need of such a God who in moments of crisis will not leave you alone, then the word about Elisha and the she-bears has much to say to you. In fact, the story is not a moral problem, instead it describes what it involves in having a God who stands by his people.

Do you see what I have done? I have not taken the story at face value nor have I rested content with time-honoured translations. I have done my own enquiry, which happily, thanks to the concordances, anybody with diligence can do, and contextualised the details. I was led step by step to the very heart of the matter and we have seen ourselves face to face with a glorious revelation of God.

Fourthly, as we come to preach from the Old Testament we are often *confused by prophetic schemes*. The Old Testament is full of expectations, and these expectations have been made the subject of so many theories, with people getting so hot under the collar about them, that we may think it is better to leave these questions alone. There is, however, a basic question raised by the prophetical schemes and it is this: how does the Old Testament envisage the development of its basic instructions? This is the question all the 'schemes' are seeking to answer – whether they put in the forefront the concept of the land or the people of God or the relationship between Israel and the world – or whatever.

Suppose, therefore, we ask a reasonably central question: what did it mean in Israel to be a believer?

Let us imagine a conversation between a typical Old Testament believer and his son. The believer has been to the altar of God with his sin offering, and has come home.

His son asks, 'Where have you been?'

'I've been to the tabernacle.'

'What did you do?'

'I brought a sin offering.'

'What did you do with it?'

'I laid my hand on the head of the beast.'

'Why did you do that?'

'Because that is the way that you appoint a substitute.'

'What did you do then?'

'I plunged the knife into it and the blood was caught by the priest.'

'Why?'

'It is symbolic of a life laid down in payment for my sin.'

'What does that mean?'

'It means that God has accepted the animal in my place and my sins have been forgiven'.

'How do you know that your sins have been forgiven?'

'Because that is what the Lord has promised.'

I suggest that this piece of imaginary conversation does, in fact, accurately represent both Old Testament thought regarding salvation and the practical, personal and religious outworking of that theology. The people of the Old Covenant, like the people of the New, were justified by faith, resting on the promises of God as those promises were expressed to them. When they offered sacrifices they were not looking forward, as if saying to themselves, 'This is a picture or shadow of the true; the perfect sacrifice is yet to come.' God's promises were given to them in relation to the sacrifices they were told to offer (Lev. 1:4; 4:20, 26, 31, 35). In the course of time, however, a genius named Isaiah was inspired by God to see that in the ultimate only a Person could fully substitute for persons (Isa. 52:13–53:12) – because (Isa. 53:7-9; Heb. 10:5-10) only a person brings to the transaction a consenting will, matching the defiled will, the central citadel and cause of sin. Consequently, when the Lord Jesus thus offered the one sacrifice for sins for ever (Heb. 10:12), he was bringing the reality of the sacrifices to their full reality. It was not that the symbolic became the literal, nor that the unreal became the true, but that reality became the full reality it was always intended to be.

So many prophetic schemes become stuck with the literal: the 'seed of Abraham' has to do with a literal family tree (notwithstanding Matthew 3:9), territorial promises must have a Palestinian fulfilment (notwithstanding John 18:36 and Hebrews 12:22), the kingdom of David must have a local throne and a worldly rule (notwithstanding Acts 15:13-18).

In this sense the relationship between the Testaments is best seen as a two-act play, wherein each act expresses valid and abiding truth in its own right; yet without Act 2 we do not know where Act 1 is going, and without Act 1 we do not know where Act 2 came from. But, taking the two Acts together, initial true reality becomes final full reality. This is how we should expound the promissory aspects of the Old Testament.

Love and Knowledge

I have spoken to you about some things which seem to me to inhibit a free and confident approach to the Old Testament on the part of preachers. I fear, however, that it may be that none of these things really touches the spot. Could it be that over and over again our uncertainty springs from the fact that we do not know the Old Testament quite as we know the New, nor give it its due importance in our Bible reading programme?

One thing is absolutely certain: facility and fluency in the pulpit in handling Scripture is fundamentally related to the quality of our personal, private walk with God in the light of his Word.

BUILDING A
CONGREGATION

Mark Ashton

7

BUILDING A CONGREGATION (1)

Mark Ashton

In addressing this important theme, I must first make clear that I do not claim to be an expert on building a congregation. Nevertheless I will endeavour to be unashamedly practical and at times personal. Please forgive me if I make my own performance sound far better than it really is. I will begin by summarising the theological assumptions with which I approach the ministry of the local church.

Theological Assumptions

(a) A God of grace who takes the initiative
There is a Creator God who acts from his own grace to reveal himself to his creatures. He always retains the initiative in his relations with us. He never allows us to wrest that initiative away from him. He sent his Son to die in order to bring us back into relationship with him, paying the price himself for our disobedience and rebellion. This saving act is mediated to us through the gospel.

(b) The gospel is prior to and defines the church
So the gospel, the message about Jesus, brings the church into existence, through the work of the Holy Spirit. The gospel is prior to the church. It calls out and defines the church. The church derives from the gospel.

When in Matthew 16 Peter confessed Jesus as 'the Christ, the Son of the living God' on the road to Caesarea Philippi, Jesus gave Peter no credit – he pointed straight to the grace of God in blessing Peter with such a revelation: 'Blessed are you, Simon son of John! For flesh and blood has not revealed this to you, but my Father in heaven.' Peter's confession was not a human achievement (flesh and blood); it was an act of divine grace. And it was on this God-given revelation of the identity of Jesus, this gospel, that Jesus would build his church. This is what constituted the rock on which the church would be built, a gospel rock, 'And I tell you, you are Peter, and on this rock I will build my church and the gates of Hades will not prevail against it.'

The structure Jesus spoke of would be a mobile and dynamic thing – something that would assault the gates of hell successfully. And Jesus made it clear that God's activity on earth would henceforth focus very specially in this church – 'I will give you the keys of the kingdom of heaven, and whatever you bind on earth shall be bound in heaven, and whatever you loose on earth shall be loosed in heaven.'

(c) *The church is to serve gospel purposes, and so is a change-enabling community*

So it is the gospel that causes the church. The church is a vehicle for the gospel to fulfil God's purposes in the world. God is determined that heaven will be populated, that he should complete the number of his elect, that there should be no empty seats around his banqueting table. It is for that purpose that he sends out his word, the gospel, and that he calls into being the church. The church exists to get people to heaven. It must therefore exist for everybody, because it is not given to us to know whom God intends to have with him in heaven. Because the gospel is a message for everybody, the church must be a community for everybody.

It is also a heaven-orientated community. It always has an eye on the future, God's future. So, on the one hand, it is always calling to those who are not yet its members to join it in order to prepare themselves for what the future holds. On the other hand, it calls on those who are its members to get themselves ready for the same future: an encounter with the absolutely holy God. It is therefore a community committed to *change* – the change of conversion in the non-member and the change of sanctification in the member. It is a *change-enabling community.*

Individually, we human beings find changing ourselves very hard. We need the help of a community – exhorting, challenging, rebuking, encouraging one another. God, in his grace, provides that community for us: a community brought about by the Word of God through the Spirit of God, shaped and directed by the Word of God, authenticated by the Word of God, and a community that gives expression to the Word of God in all that it does. (Notice that there is no distinction between the work of the Holy Spirit and the work of the Word of God.)

There, for what they are worth, are my theological assumptions about the church: A God of grace, whose gospel brings the church into being, in order to get people to heaven. So how are we to understand the role of the minister, the church leader, in the light of that?

The pastor's role in building a congregation

(a) The pastor's priorities

The pastor's highest priority is to be a servant of the Word of God, because to be a servant of the Word of God is, as we have already seen, to be a servant of God. And serving God must come before serving the congregation, because the only effective way we *can* serve the congregation is by serving God. It is *his* community. It does not exist in its own right; and it certainly is not my community. Diplomacy has been well defined as 'the art of letting other people have my own way'. But church leadership is an altogether different matter. I do not build a congregation. I cannot. God alone does that. And it is my task to keep myself very close to him.

I like to quote Matthew 4:4 ('Man shall not live by bread alone but by every word that comes out of the mouth of God') to encourage myself in my preaching. But I need to be reminded that it is not just the congregation who are kept

alive spiritually by the Bible. I too will die physically
without physical food and spiritually without the Word of
God. So, I must guard my own 'times of quiet' jealously –
against the incursions and demands of my own ministry (not
using them to do the Bible study for my preaching), and even
against my own family (knowing that the greatest thing I can
do for each member of my family every day is to keep myself
very close to God).

I must myself be taught, if I would teach others. God wants
to speak to me as me, not just as husband, father, pastor or
church leader, but as his own child, with no role or
responsibility coming between him and me.

But, if my first priority is to God alone, my second priority
is to my wife and my family. I cannot neglect them and be a
faithful pastor of a church. It is easy to jump straight from my
own devotional life with God to my public ministry, without
passing through the necessary circles of biblical priority that
lie between. You can picture them as a series of concentric
rings, with God at the centre, my spouse in the first ring, my
children in the next, my colleagues in the one beyond, and so
on. Paul is quite clear in instructing Timothy and Titus that
the marriage and the family life of the church leader is highly
relevant to his public ministry. There should be no conflict
here. The way I pastor my congregation is by being the best
husband and father I can be. We reach the outer rings via the
inner rings.

I try to remind myself regularly that the spiritual well-
being of my wife and family are more important than my
ministry to St. Andrew the Great. I would resign from the
ordained ministry if it threatened the health of my marriage.
It is important for my wife to know that. I try to be very strict
in keeping to one day off in every seven. For myself (and I
am not implying this is necessarily right for others) on any
day I try to take on no work commitments between five and
eight in the evening – a poor time for ministry and a pressure
time for wives and children at home: they need me then.

Such a priority does not make a minister worse at his job, because the time we invest in our marriages and in our families pays us back with increased energy for ministry; indeed it is an integral part of a well-rounded ministry. Few things damage our spiritual lives so effectively as marital conflict (1 Pet. 3:7).

If we are to be faithful servants of the Word, then we must keep ourselves close to God (humble, attentive and obedient to his Word), and we must attend to our own marriages and families.

But *priorities* imply *posteriorities*. I cannot put certain things at the top of the list without inevitably putting other things at the bottom of the list. For some of us the difficulty is not in deciding what things we should do, but in deciding what things we should *not* do. One missionary had a little plaque above his desk with the words 'Planned Neglect' on it. When asked to explain it, he would say that there were many worthy and excellent things in life that he planned to neglect in order to focus his time and energy on those things that he deemed to be of the highest priority.

We need to know what we should *not* be doing. We need to pray for the wisdom to discern this correctly and for the courage to direct our lives accordingly, in face of the unpopularity that will inevitably occur. But we also need to make sure that it is we ourselves who pay the first and highest price for our own self-discipline. It is possible to be self-disciplined and to adhere to priorities at the expense of others. We can use the priority of a preaching ministry as an excuse to retreat into our studies and to evade responsibilities that we should fulfil. I need to be reminded that I go into my study only in order to get into the pulpit. I am not my own master, indulging myself in the luxury of uninterrupted Bible study. I am a servant of the Word *and* of the church. I attend to the one in order to attend to the other. My time is not my own, to allocate as I choose. It belongs to Another and he commands me to lay it down for the service of the

congregation in the most effective way. I go into the study in
order to reach the pulpit.

So my priorities in ministry must not become an excuse
for laziness, for self-indulgence, or for evading pastoral
responsibilities. Let me be sure that it is not others who have
to pay the price for my inefficiency disguised as single-
mindedness. That is not the application of godly priorities –
it is selfishness.

On the other hand, what I believe about the nature of
ministry ought to shape the way I live out my ministry. I
ought to control my own diary so that it does reflect my
priorities each week: do I let my diary get filled with people
booking me up? Or do I take the initiative in booking up the
people whom I think I ought to be seeing in a particular week?
Do I block out the necessary preparation time every week so
that it does not get filled with other things? I must let what I
believe fill my life, because there are so many other things
that will fill my life the moment I drop my guard in this
respect. We need to share our priorities with our
congregations, so that they are aware of them, and agree with
them, and help us to stick to them.

And it is not bad and shameful things that will threaten
our highest priorities most effectively. The greatest threat
will come from things that are good and worthy in themselves,
things that have a high moral value, but things that are not
what God means me to focus my time and attention on now.
In any list of priorities the greatest threat to number one
priority is not posed by the things at the very bottom of the
list. It comes from number two priority. The devil knows all
too well that it is much easier to sow confusion in our minds
about the many good and worthy claims on our time, than it
is to persuade us to pass our hours in betting shops or wine
bars. Only prayer and clear thinking will allow us to discern
God's will for us, so that we can judge rightly between good
things that we should not be doing (however popular they
might make us with other people) and good things that we

should be doing because they are God's priorities for us.

In considering this topic of *Building a Congregation*, I want to urge us as ministers to start with ourselves, by reviewing our own priorities. Our task is to teach people the Word of God in order that they may minister it to others. To do that, our own lives must reflect the order of priorities that we really believe in, so that people can both *hear* and *see* our message.

(b) The pastor's responsibilities

(i) Unity

It is our task in our churches to have a deep concern for their unity. I have heard what the New Testament has to say on the subject of unity applied a great deal to wider issues of ecumenism. But verses like Ephesians 4:3 (*maintain the unity of the Spirit in the bond of peace*) did not have unity between different Christian denominations as their initial focus. It was the local congregation that was in view, and that is where concern for Christian unity must start.

It is not my task to divide the local church. The pastor does not change the church effectively by dividing it. But on the other hand there is always the potential for division when the church changes (and, according to my theological assumptions, the healthy biblical church will always be changing). So the minister has a responsibility to maintain unity in the face of possible division.

This will influence the pace of change, and it highlights the need for good communication within the congregation. It is necessary for the leadership of a church to work hard to communicate their vision effectively to the whole fellowship. The pace of change must be limited by the speed and ability of the fellowship to understand, absorb and own that vision.

But the communication flow runs the other way, too. Leaders have to learn to listen to what the Spirit is saying to the church. I do not believe I have any monopoly of vision.

Indeed, in my experience, most initiatives in the life of my local church have not been started by me. It has often been my task as a leader to find out where the people of the church are going, and then to walk in front of them!

Of course, we are in it together. In many cases I would find it very hard to say where an idea in our church had originated. But one test to apply in order to see whether any particular idea is from God, is to see whether the congregation unites around it. If it divides rather than unites, warning bells should start ringing.

As pastors, we must learn how to listen. Finding out why people do what they do, what makes them tick, is particularly important in taking on a new pastoral responsibility. It is the preacher's task to listen to the congregation. He knows what he is trying to say to them, as he teaches the Bible week by week. But he must listen to them in order to hear what they are learning from the Spirit through the Word week by week. The Spirit is a Spirit of unity. He does not tear the flock of Christ apart, and we should take care that we do not either.

(ii) Vision and planning

Discerning and communicating vision are delicate tasks if we would maintain unity. But they are necessary for the life of the church. God himself is a planner with a plan for the universe (see Eph. 1:3-14). His plan provides us with a vision of where we are going and what we will become. Without that vision the people of God will be in danger of perishing along the way (Prov. 29:18), because from our viewpoint the present is difficult and the future is dark.

So we plan because God has a future and a hope for us (Jer. 29:11). Our planning is not aimed at our own goals but at his. In planning, we endeavour to cast a net over the future to bring about the fulfilment of God's goals. But we have to recognise how weak and sinful our planning processes will always be – partly because we have a great way of substituting our own goals for his, partly because the future is quite unknown to us and we do not know what each day will bring forth, and partly because we should never underestimate our own inability to carry out well-laid and wise plans.

But we cannot evade the task of planning. It is the minister's job to unite the fellowship round a vision of what God wants to do in and through them, individually and corporately, and to work out that vision in practical, immediate steps. Those steps must be kept under constant review, always open to objection and correction. The habit of an older generation of evangelicals of adding 'DV' (God willing) to remarks about the future was a godly one (reflecting Jas. 4:13-17).

So we need humility and prayer for our planning. And we also need that wider, divine perspective provided by scripture. God's perspective is wider than ours and his timescale is longer than ours, a lot longer. We so easily overestimate what we can achieve in six months, but underestimate what we can achieve in five years.

On page 131 there is a draft vision document with which we work in our fellowship. It is nothing very special. But it will show you how we start the planning process. We do not claim to be good at it, but we are aware of its importance. Since I came to the Round Church at St. Andrew the Great, I have prayed virtually every day in the terms of Solomon's prayer that God would give me a heart of wisdom to discern between good and evil in order to govern the people well (1 Kgs. 3:9). Wisdom *for* the church is my daily need as a pastor.

(iii) Administration

It is popular today to despise administration, particularly as an enemy of preaching. Administration *per se* is not an enemy of preaching, but bad administration is. The growth of the local church is as effectively checked by incompetent administration as it is by wrong priorities in the life of the minister. A super-spiritual attitude here may just be another excuse for laziness and selfishness, and it may well set a limit to the development of a congregation.

There is also in me – and I suspect in others – a longing for the alchemist's stone in administration: a quick-fire short cut that will cut through all the problems, deal with all the backlogs, and solve all the hassles. I am beginning to suspect that such a thing does not exist. The solution to administration does not lie in adopting any particular technique. We have to steel ourselves to what is palpably obvious from the pages of the New Testament: the call to full-time ministry is a call to hard work. If the minister is going to maintain his priorities, he will have to work hard to keep administrative tasks in their place, or, like a Russian Vine, they will overrun and tangle up the rest of his life.

It is important, therefore, to apportion to them the appropriate amount of time and then to do them with the maximum energy and concentration. For some the temptation will be to get too absorbed in them and to become proud of our administrative machismo. Others make the opposite boast, claiming in effect to be too spiritual for such mundane work. For many of us the temptation will be to delay those tasks we do not enjoy until they loom over us like guilt-laden thunderclouds, having grown to quite unmanageable proportions. If you want a slogan: 'Kill your administration before your administration kills you.'

Answering correspondence, filing, service preparation, long-term planning, committee paperwork, overseeing secretarial staff: there is a right proportion of our time to spend on all of these. The secret, if there is one, seems to me to be judging what that proportion should be and sticking to it ruthlessly. Somebody once told me to do early in the day the task I most dread: I think it was good advice and I pass it on for what it is worth. Winston Churchill said that men who change the world have generally done so by lunchtime.

The task of running a living church will frequently defeat us. We will be brought to our knees. Particularly if the church grows, we may sense that we are getting out of our depth.

But I guess that being out of my depth may be the only safe position from which to lead a church. If it is God's church and he builds it, I need to guard myself constantly against trying to take that initiative away from him. Any sense of competence, of being adequate for the task, may be dangerous. The church is the outworking of God's grace from beginning to end; and the pastor, just like every other Christian (assuming he is one), is a miracle of that grace too.

It is the grace of God that builds the church, not human achievement. We depend on that grace. Everything in church leadership that humbles me, that teaches me that I am not adequate to the tasks before me, that throws me back on my knees in prayer to God, is to be welcomed. My greatest enemy here is that proud self-sufficiency that is always urging me to rely on myself. So a sense of despair at the administrative burdens of church leadership may be quite healthy, so long as it leads us to pray and to work hard at administration within strict limits.

(c) The pastor's focus

We have already seen the pressing need for priorities in our ministry, priorities which reflect what God has told us of his will for us in the Bible. As ministers we are servants of God's Word. And I must organise my life so that it expresses that. I must strive to be the most effective teacher of God's Word that I can be. That will mean that I guard jealously the best possible times of the week for sermon preparation. But the sermon is not the only way the Bible is taught in the local church.

There are also the smaller groups that meet in homes for Bible study and discussion. I hope that my experience is unusual, but I have to say I have not been encouraged by the level of Bible study that seems to go on in most home groups. At St. Andrew the Great I struggled for six years with this, trying to train and resource home group leaders, with little success. So we made a new senior staff appointment with the specific brief to raise the level of Bible learning that occurred in the home groups. Our strategy is to focus more staff resources on the leaders as a key to lifting the groups from the sharing of ignorances (at their worst heretical and at their best 'blessed thoughts') towards more edifying, theologically informed discussion.

But there is a need to focus our ministry more sharply still, from the congregation to the cell group, to the individual. It is striking how narrowly Jesus focused his ministry. He concentrated on the Jews largely to the exclusion of Gentiles. He used parables to sieve out from among his casual listeners those with a genuine interest (Mark 4:11). From his serious followers, he picked seventy to send out; but from within the seventy he had a prior commitment to twelve; and even within the twelve he chose three to accompany him at a number of key moments: the raising of Jairus's daughter, the transfiguration, Gethsemane. Even within those three Jesus singled out Peter for special attention (and perhaps also 'the disciple whom Jesus loved'). Undoubtedly, Jesus could have influenced more people – many more were eager to come within his orbit – but there was a clear focus to his ministry. He worked outwards from strength, building up one or two of a small inner group, and then the twelve and, from that unlikely beginning, founding the church that has spread throughout the world. No single life has been as effective as his in impacting the whole human race.

The early years of my own ministry were transformed when I suddenly realised that I would influence deeply the lives of only a few people during my first full-time post. Up to then I was deluding myself that I was influencing the whole of a largish church. Management experts talk of the 'Pareto principle' – twenty per cent of our work will achieve eighty per cent of our results. There is no particular biblical/spiritual wisdom in that, but it is a shrewd observation of how things are in life. We would do well to ponder what significance that has for our own ministries.

We will only be able to invest deeply in the lives of a few other people. Our public preaching and teaching will be for all. Our planning of programmes and of structures and of staffing for the church will benefit all. But we also have the opportunity to give ourselves deeply at a personal level to just a few folk. We should pick those people carefully. Jesus spent a night in prayer before calling the twelve (and the inclusion of Judas Iscariot should guard us against any unwarranted perfectionism in this).

It is sometimes said that the minister cannot have really close friends in his own congregation. I can make no biblical sense of that at all. Indeed it seems to me to lie at the root of all sorts of problems, and potential problems, in pastoral ministry. The pastor *must* be pastored by his own congregation. Which is not to say that love, support and oversight from outside the congregation are not also to be welcomed. Of course they are. But if we see ourselves as discipling our churches but not ourselves being discipled by them, the relationship is dangerously unhealthy. We cannot have really deep relationships with everyone within the church. But we must have really deep relationships with some of them.

From these deep personal relationships we will ourselves receive love, support, encouragement, admonition, rebuke, exhortation. These relationships will also be one of the most effective aspects of our teaching ministry, as we work one-to-one with a few other people and impact their lives at a much deeper level than we can with the rest of the congregation. As with other priorities in the life of the minister, these relationships will not make our wider ministry to the whole fellowship less effective. Developed under the guidance and in the power of the Spirit, they are the arteries that link us to the whole body. They keep us spiritually healthy, and they keep our ministry spiritually healthy.[1]

A realistic focus in our ministries is as important as gospel priorities. It guards us both from the guilt of feeling that we ought to be blessing every member of the church to the same extent all the time, and from the delusion of thinking that we are. When we consider Jesus's ministry, we realise that this is not just pragmatism; it is his own pattern.

In this matter of Building a Congregation we as leaders start, then, with ourselves: with our *theology*, reminding ourselves that the work is God's from start to finish; with our *priorities* – to put God first in our own lives and to guard our marriages and families; with our *responsibilities* – to maintain unity, impart vision, and oil the wheels of the fellowship with our own hard work at administration; and with our *focus*, in developing deep personal friendships with a focused few.

---

1. We will want to have the same focus in our personal evangelism, so that we develop deep and lasting relationships with some non-Christians and endeavour to present Jesus to them in the context of serious and extended personal friendship. I have never found 'full-time' Christian service a disadvantage for befriending non-Christians. One does not need to be exposed to a large number of non-Christian contacts in the workplace each day to have strong friendships with as many non-Christians as it is possible to evangelise effectively at any one time. We should be modelling personal evangelism in our everyday lives in this way for the benefit of others in the church who are starting to learn to evangelise for themselves.

Our Vision for the
Round Church at St. Andrew the Great

A church committed to the Bible and to Prayer

At the heart of our ministry is teaching the Bible as God's key instrument for proclaiming Jesus Christ as Lord and for building up his followers on earth.

Our worship is the offering of our entire lives to God in holiness and service. At our main meetings we aim (1) to encourage each other to feed ourselves on God's word and to give ourselves to prayer, so that we may worship God better in our lives; and (2) to draw in outsiders without embarrassment.

A church committed to a specific mission

It is our special task to serve the university community in which we are placed. There are two aspects to the work of our church ('Town' and 'Gown'), but both depend on one another: by becoming a better 'normal' church, we also become a better student church.

A church committed to mature discipleship for every member

Some people are paid to organise the church's life, but all are ministers of the gospel. So we also meet in smaller groups to encourage one another to identify our spiritual gifts and to use them to serve others. Each member should have a vision of what God wants to do with his or her life for his own glory.

We believe that God means us to grow, individually and as a church; that growth is change; and that change may be painful. We accept the pain of change gladly for the sake of bringing the gospel to our contemporaries.

8

BUILDING A CONGREGATION (2)

Mark Ashton

The previous chapter covered my theological assumptions and the role of the minister (his priorities, responsibilities and focus). In this chapter I will consider ten aspects of church life, some in more detail than others. At times I will lapse from reasoned discourse into more of a series of disjointed observations about an aspect of church life. But I hope that what I write does follow from the theological assumptions outlined in the previous chapter.

1. Growing the church

It is fundamental to our understanding of the church that it is not a mere human community. It is a community brought into existence by the Word of God. It is Jesus Christ who builds his church. It is not skilful church leaders who engineer church growth. God's grace has the initiative, and God never lets go of that initiative and never allows it to fall into human hands.

If the church is a living manifestation of God's grace, then human merit does not have a part to play in building it up. When some organisation tells us how a particular church has adopted a particular strategy and has grown tenfold – or a hundredfold or a thousandfold! – in consequence, we should be moved to praise the grace of God, not to rush out to emulate the method in expectation of similar growth ourselves. God's grace means that he blesses us despite what we are and do, not because of it. If a church is growing, it is because God is being good to it despite all its sin and failures: it is not because it has suddenly struck upon the right method for church growth.

What God is doing is not easily visible to human eyes. So

not all visible, numerical growth in a church will necessarily be his work. Our criterion for judging any strategy for the church must be its faithfulness to what he has said to us in the Bible, not whether it adds to our numbers. All church growth methodologies and the 'church leadership by statistical analysis' that are popular today must be subject to this caveat. *We* do not grow the church or build the congregation, and, while we think we can, we probably get in the way of the only One who actually can.

But if it is Christ's intention to build his church, then we can pray that he will do so. And prayer is exactly the right attitude to the growth of the church. We cannot have a five-year plan for it as though we can achieve it ourselves. It is not a human achievement. But we can pray for it as God has made his will clear in the matter. And then we can expect it as we expect answers to all our prayers, trusting God to act in his own way and in his own time, for our best interests. I think there is an important distinction between seeing church growth as something we achieve by 'getting things right' (by our clear thinking and our hard work), and seeing church growth as something God grants as and when he chooses.

I was deeply struck once to hear Bishop Frank Retief of South Africa speak of the spectacular growth of his own congregation and then its decline without any hint of pride or of regret. At one time God blessed them with rapid growth and at another he allowed the numbers to decrease, but Frank Retief's concern throughout was that they should be faithful and obedient to the Word of God, not that they should be 'successful'. How often have you heard a church leader with that strong a theology? When told we should 'plan for growth' I like to alter two letters and 'pray for growth'. Our guideline for the future development of our churches should not be 'How can I increase the size of this church?' but 'How can I bring this church more into line with the will of God, so that he can fulfil his purposes for her?' It is only as we answer that question that we will get our planning for growth right.

2. Assembling the church

The answer to the question in the previous paragraph is 'by teaching the church the Word more faithfully and more humbly'. As it is the Word of God that brings the church into existence, it is the ministry of the Word that is the wellspring and centre of the church's life. In fact the church in its local manifestation *is* the group of people who assemble around the ministry of the Word in a particular place. So our weekly meetings are for us to meet one another under the ministry of the Word of God. We must consider the importance and the purpose of those meetings or assemblies.

They are important because they are what defines the church. The Round Church at St. Andrew the Great in Cambridge would continue to exist as a church if all its organisations and programmes closed down, if all its staff were sacked, if all its property were sold, so long as a group of people continued to gather on a Sunday morning to hear the Word of God. I plan my week's work around that fact.

Nothing is more important in the structured life of the Round Church than its Sunday services. They are its main Bible study, prayer meeting, fellowship gathering. They are the main time when the diverse needs of its members can be met. Structurally everything else spins off from this centre. So the preparation of the Sunday services is very important indeed. All in all as much of our staff time goes into the preparing of the Sunday meetings as goes into the preparing of the sermons. The senior staff have an extended meeting every Monday afternoon to de-brief the previous Sunday and to plan the services for the coming Sundays.

We try to communicate to the congregation a sense of the importance of the Sunday meetings. As Christians we can underestimate our need for regular encouragement in the faith. The vital result of every Sunday service is that we are each helped to go on believing in God for one more week (Isa. 50:4). However far we have travelled in the Christian life, we need that help. Other meetings during the week cannot take the place of the Sunday services (and shouldn't be allowed to).

This helps us to understand the purpose of assembling the church. It is not for worship. Not directly. Which is why the New Testament does not use 'worship' language for the assembling of believers. It uses 'edification' language. We come together to build one another up in our faith and to do those things together that we cannot do apart. But it is not our meetings that constitute our grateful response to God for his grace to us, i.e. our 'worship', our mirroring back to him what he is worth. It has to be our whole lives that do that. When we start to talk about church services as 'worship' we don't just get our understanding of the purpose and nature of services hopelessly confused, we run the danger of failing to understand what all human life is about. It may be a vain plea, but I do wish we would stop restricting the use of the word 'worship' to what we do in church. It is making our attitude to our assemblies one of pagan superstition, and it is encouraging us to understand our lives and our careers in a humanist and secular way. That is an issue bigger than I can address here, but trying to understand our Sunday services in strictly New Testament terms leads us at St. Andrew the Great to what we call the four Es as the controlling guidelines for service planning.

The first, as you have guessed, is *edification*. To put it negatively, nothing should happen at a church service that tends to the dismantling and discouragement of faith. We have met to build one another up, young and old, rich and poor, clever and simple. So we keep asking ourselves about every aspect of the service, 'Will this edify those who are there? Will it help them to go on believing that there is a God who loves them? Will it encourage them to live holy lives and to serve other people this coming week?'

Embarrassment is the great enemy of edification. It may be especially true of British culture, but once a Briton is embarrassed, nothing valuable goes on inside that individual until the embarrassment is removed. Will this greeting, this song, this prayer, these notices, this testimony embarrass anyone? Will someone be feeling uncomfortable if we do things that way? If you want to maximise edification, minimise embarrassment.

I once attended a student church in a different culture, where the service leader asked newcomers to identify themselves at the beginning of the service by raising a hand so that they could be specially greeted and handed a welcome pack by the stewards. He went on to say that if any of us were regulars but suspected that a newcomer sitting next to us was too shy to raise his or her hand at that point, we were to raise our hand for them and point at them, so that the stewards could identify them. This was not a British way of doing things!

A clue to minimising embarrassment in the church service is the pursuit of *excellence*. Even though an item in a service may not suit my taste, the better it is done the less uncomfortable I will feel about it. We cannot suit every taste present in our fellowship in everything we do (nor should we – indeed it would for me be a bad sign if someone leaving a service thanked me and said, 'Every aspect of that service was exactly how I would have wanted it to be'). No, every service ought to be a mixture of tastes, challenging all of us to make greater allowances for the tastes and preferences of others. But we can do everything we do to the best of our ability. That honours God; it emphasises the importance of our meeting together as a fellowship; and it minimises embarrassment.

This link between edification, embarrassment and excellence, is the same for a fourth E – *evangelism*. There is no sharp distinction to be drawn between edification and evangelism at Sunday services. Both are achieved by the meeting together of God's people humbly and attentively under his Word in a way that pursues excellence and removes embarrassment. Our Sunday services are the most effective evangelism we do at St. Andrew the Great. We seek to provide services to which Christians can easily invite their friends, at which the friends will not be embarrassed and at which they will be able to get to grips with Christianity. It is not that what we do will necessarily be familiar to them. How common an activity is community singing in our culture now? But it will be apparent to a guest that we are in earnest.

There should be no doubt of the seriousness of what we are about. Nor of its accessibility. The outsider may not agree with the Christian faith, but he or she must be able to see that it matters a very great deal to us, and that we are speaking about it in terms that are intelligible to him or to her. As we preach our way through the various books of the Bible Sunday by Sunday, we try to make sure in our sermons that we let the non-Christian know that we know that he or she is there. So the non-Christian does not feel like an interloper eavesdropping on a meeting of an esoteric sect, but is reassured that it is all right to be there as someone who has not yet decided about Jesus Christ for himself or herself.

We have occasional guest services and very occasional missions, but it is my hunch that the bulk of our evangelism goes on at the regular week by week Sunday services. We want the whole congregation to have confidence in those services and to see them as a natural part of their own evangelism.

The music at our services is constantly controlled by the four Es – edification and evangelism being the ends, and the removal of embarrassment and the pursuit of excellence being the means to those ends. Because we are serious about what we are doing at our services, we can never take lightly the words we sing. Voltaire once said, 'If a thing is too silly to be said, it can always be sung'. As we know, some Christian songs merit that verdict. So we try to survey in advance every word of every song we sing, and to make adjustments where necessary. The overriding purpose of the whole service is not the precise statement of doctrine; it is edification and evangelism. But, if it is the Word of God that brings the church about, builds it up, and adds to its numbers, then it is our task to be faithful and as accurate as we can in communicating that Word. Sometimes a careful introduction is required just to set a song in a correct theological framework. If the music and the singing are not controlled by the four Es, they will tend either to be embarrassingly bad or to dominate the meeting inappropriately. It is as dangerous to underestimate as it is to overestimate the part music plays in our meetings.

Another major issue in assembling the church is how to edify and evangelise all the different ages. I have noticed that the crèche and the Sunday School (though we try to avoid using that term) play a major role in evangelism. In our child-centred society, young parents are usually happy if their children are happy. But they will rarely start coming to church if their children are not happy to attend. Moreover, the Bible provides us with little warrant for evangelising other people's children (despite all the Christian energies over the years that have gone into that form of evangelism), but it does give us plenty of encouragement for edifying and evangelising the whole family (the whole household) together. So it is important to think in terms of whole families.

The value of the united Family Service – when all ages (bar the crèche) stay together throughout the service – should not be underrated. Although all parts of such a service must be child-friendly (it is not fair to keep the children in and then to ignore them), they do not have to be child*ish*. A shorter, simplified and illustrated sermon can edify and evangelise adults effectively. Indeed it may be more effective because it is the medium and not the message that has been adjusted. Spiritual truth is not appropriated intellectually by human beings. Adult cognitive processes are not necessary for feeding in depth on the Word of God. But, if a Family Service talk is going to edify the whole family, the preacher will need to prepare as seriously as he would for a full-length adult sermon. More of our time may have to go on the medium of communication, and more of our time will certainly have to go on the painful business of what to leave out, but we can never let ourselves think that it is 'only a children's talk this week'. Great simplicity requires great clarity of thought, and that will require the sort of deep understanding of the passage that comes only through hard preparation.

It is probably true that adults may sometimes learn more when they don't think they are themselves being directly addressed in the sermon. Their guard is down when they feel like spectators watching the speaker talk to the children. Nevertheless I believe it is a mistake to encourage the congregation to think in those terms about a Family Service talk. The children have a greater need to know that the Bible is being taken seriously by their parents and by the rest of the adults of the church, than the adults have a need to watch the Bible being taught to the children. The Bible is not a book of morals for teaching our children how to behave properly: it is a book by which all believers live. It is vitally important that the children of the church see the adults of the church being taught the Bible and bringing their lives under it. So at the Round we encourage our preachers to speak directly and specifically to the adults from time to time in Family Services, and to let the children know they are doing so. In that way there can be no doubt in anyone's mind as to how seriously we *all* take the Bible.

As a church we have not tried an all-age Sunday School, so I will not comment on that pattern of Sunday meetings. I do not believe that there is only one way we can meet on Sundays, but I am sure that the assembling of the church week by week is the very centre of its life. It is for that reason that I have spent so long on this heading (without in any way exhausting it). But we must now move on.

3. Building the church

While the main weekly meetings are at the centre of edification and evangelism in the local church, edification and evangelism are not confined to those gatherings. Teaching the Word of God will occur in many different forms.

The moment we use the word 'teaching', there is a danger that we start to think about the church's work in exclusively educational terms. Although the New Testament does use educational language about ministry, we should not allow modern educational philosophy to dominate our thinking. The language of *feeding* is also prevalent in the New Testament. So to assess the calibre of a sermon by asking how accurately a member of the congregation can recall its teaching points may be a bit like suggesting that a meal does not do us good unless we can recall the precise menu. I cannot remember the menus of the meals I ate last year, but I doubt I would be here now if I had not eaten them. The Word of God feeds us spiritually. That process cannot be analysed in purely educational terms. It is not open to merely intellectual examination. But it is what keeps us spiritually alive.

The insights of modern educational theory are therefore of only limited value in helping us to plan the life of the local church. For example, it is a fallacy to think that I am only learning spiritually when I am learning something new. There are many Bible truths we need to return to over and over again (2 Pet. 1:12-15). It is also important that any increase in spiritual knowledge is expressed in a changed life. Enabling change is the business of the church. We need to have the highest faith in preaching as God's ordained way of building the church *and* to pursue all other methods of bringing the Word of God to bear on the people of God. I referred in the previous chapter to the cell-group life of the church. While I believe the home group Bible studies to be secondary to the Sunday meetings, they are clearly enormously important, and warrant careful planning and resourcing.

I also mentioned the focus of our lives in ministry in deep

relationships with a few. These are the people who will know us really well and who will be learning as much from our lives as they learn from our lips. But in my ministry I am also searching for ways of pastoring the congregation in general that are effective in bringing individuals and families under the Word of God. Richard Baxter in *The Reformed Pastor* provided a model of catechising whole families as he visited systematically in his Kidderminster parish. Wallace Benn has worked out the same principles to a different pattern in the Orthos Booklet, *The Baxter Model*.

I have to say that I, like Wallace and unlike Richard Baxter, am dubious of the value of door-to-door visitation, in our culture today. It was what I was made to cut my teeth on at the outset of my own ministry, and it was certainly a valuable training exercise. No doubt many of us here have vivid memories of nightmare pastoral visits.

I am not convinced that visiting is now as effective for evangelism or for pastoral care as it may once have been. We need to find ways that are equivalent to Richard Baxter's catechising of the families of Kidderminster, but that suit our society today. Opportunities arise through requests for baptisms and marriage preparation to teach the Bible to couples and families. The exposition of scripture must be at the heart of what we're doing, and pastoral counselling must be directed to that. We have to learn to develop the ability to apply the Bible's teaching to the situation of an individual or a family. Some of us are strong on the former skill, but weak on the latter.

The appointment of a leader to some part of the church is also a good moment for going over the basics. When interviewing someone about leadership, we use a questionnaire form at St. Andrew the Great that covers such areas as testimony to conversion, understanding of the gospel and ability to explain it, private Bible reading and prayer, church attendance, financial giving, family prayers, appetite for Christian service. This allows a member of the church's staff to do a spiritual check-up on an individual, which might be awkward to set up in any other way. It is also a good time to share a mission statement for the church with the individual, so that all those who are appointed to leadership are familiar with and in agreement with the church's basic vision.

But the top priority in all such situations is to teach the Bible (particularly the Bible basics), because the church is built by the exposition of the Word.

4. Changing the church

The church is all about change: the change of conversion and the change of sanctification (getting ready for heaven). It is God's grace through his Word that brings about such change, and it is the task of ministry to bring that Word to bear on human lives and to help it to do its changing work.

So it is in the pastor's heart that change in the local church begins. We must ourselves be people who are living under the reproving, correcting, exhorting Word of God. If we cannot change (and be seen to change in ways that are costly to us personally), we cannot expect our churches to change. About the only poor piece of advice that I received from my first Vicar (to whom I owe an immense amount) was his insistence that you should never be seen to change your mind in public. I now believe that to be wrong.

The minister will need a reserve of energy in order to pastor a changing church. Change is emotionally expensive for all concerned. Time is required to ponder, to pray and to weigh alternatives. What in management terms is known as 'walking the floor' will also be needed, to get a feel of how others in the church see a situation and to understand their (possibly strongly held) opinions. While the desire for popularity is a bad guideline for change, ignorance of what other people think is equally damaging to healthy change.

We all have 'comfort zones' around us. Things that come inside my comfort zone, I am happy about; things outside it disturb and unsettle me. It is the task of the church leadership to widen the comfort zones of members of the fellowship by introducing change at a pace that allows an idea to move gradually from the outside to the inside of their comfort zones. Leadership by surprise is a fatal strategy in the life of the local church. I have watched church leaders shoot themselves in the foot by springing a new idea on an eldership group without warning, pressing for an immediate verdict on it, and being surprised at the very frosty reception it gets.

We may have been tempted sometimes to lament at the phenomenon of 'custard Christians', those who get upset over trifles. But it may be that the pace of change has been mishandled by the leadership and that has been the cause of an outbreak of what one friend calls 'pewmoania'. In a perfect world a new plan ought first to appear on any group's agenda only as an information item, just to be taken note of. At the group's next meeting, it appears for discussion; and only on the third agenda does it come up for decision. By removing the decision from the discussion, you maximise the light and minimise the heat. You also provide the necessary space for people to change their minds. Every group divides itself into 'early-adopters' of new ideas, 'opinion-leaders' (whose support for any development is vital to its success), and 'hold-outs' (on whom it is important not to slam the door: go on giving them chances to opt in long after the rest of the church has pressed ahead).

Local churches will inevitably have different characteristics and will develop in different ways. It is important for a congregation to know which way their own church is going. A church should be clear about where it is going, and then it is fair to hope for unity of purpose in the congregation. It will be our aim to pastor churches that are clearly going in a gospel direction, with our congregations aware of that and committed to it.

The management of change is a fruitful study for the church leader as he seeks to press home the application of the Word of God and to maintain the unity of the fellowship at the same time.

5. Leading the church

Helping the church to change is a part of leadership that may cause us to think in terms of the individual visionary leader who received the vision, communicates the vision, and motivates others to pursue the vision. I hope I have already said enough to make it clear that, while God repeatedly uses individuals to achieve his purposes, the leadership of the local church is always corporate. But there is a strong human tendency towards clericalism, the desire to put someone up on a pedestal – in order either to hero worship him, or to knock him. We must guard against clericalism: not just because of the unreasonable expectations it places on the individual church leader, who may try to act the Jack-of-all-Trades the congregation wants him to be, but because of what it does for the congregation's role in the life of the church.

The church leader must come down off the pedestal and put himself alongside the rest of the fellowship. Even when preaching it is important to remind the congregation that, while it is our duty to teach them the Bible faithfully and accurately in the assembly, it is their duty to check that we are doing it correctly. So they will need to study their own Bibles and they will need the courage to question us about our exposition. We will need the humility to admit where we have been wrong. I have had to apologise for the previous week's sermon, and even once had to apologise before the end of a service. I probably should have done that more often than I have.

The teaching of the Bible is not the leader's preserve. It is the task of the whole congregation. It is not confined to the pulpit. It goes on at every level of the church's life. That is the priesthood of all believers in practice.

Some people are paid to organise the church's life and to be freed to teach the Bible publicly in the assembly. But all Christians are ministers of the gospel. It is the privilege and responsibility of every Christian to teach others about God. We must not let our people start to think that organising the church's life and taking decisions in church matters is ministry. It is a chore for servant leaders. Indeed it is the task of the leadership to keep the chores of organising and leading the church away from the majority of the congregation, so that they can be free for ministry. It is a great pity when people think that sitting on committees, taking decisions, and organising are at the top of a hierarchy of ministry. There is no hierarchy of ministry, but, if there were, such things would scarcely feature on the list.

We must teach that, and act that way. The ministry of the church is conducted by the people of the church. So when we are considering a new initiative in the life of the church (for example, shall we start a mums and toddlers programme? or shall we open a drop-in centre for the unemployed?); the first issue to address is not whether such a programme is desirable, but whether God has provided us with the people who have the vision and the capabilities to run it. In the local church you can only do that for which God has provided the necessary people. So that also means stopping some activities when the key people leave. The leadership must be people-orientated, rather than programme-orientated.

We must encourage all the church members to think ambitiously about how they can each minister the gospel themselves. They will need first to know the gospel for themselves, to be confident about explaining it to others, and then to look for ways in which they can be effective in building up other Christians and in evangelising non-Christians. To achieve this it may be necessary to reduce the activity base of our churches. Too much local church life is run on guilt. It is the task of leadership to reduce guilt in the lives of the members of the church. As grace, not merit, is the heart of our theology, so gratitude, not guilt, is the heart of our ethics (our behaviour).

So it may well be that we ought to be telling some of our members to be less involved in the life of the church rather than more involved. At St. Andrew the Great we have concentrated regular church meetings onto two nights of the week: committees meet only on Monday nights, and the mid-week Bible study groups only meet on Wednesdays. While this causes some problems, it has the great advantage of preventing the church's activities from spreading right through the week for some of the most committed members of the congregation.

We also try to limit church involvement in a way appropriate to a person's life-stage. I challenge the graduate who has just finished his or her studies to get more involved in the life of a local church. But I ask newly-weds to take a complete year off from caring for other people spiritually within the structured programmes of the church (so that they can devote all their emotional energies to getting to know one another and to building a stable marriage relationship that will last the distance). But once that twelve months is over, we look to draw them back in to the programmes. Parents of young children need to be freed from church responsibilities in order to concentrate on the nurture of their families at home (particularly as this stage may coincide with career pressures), but as the children leave home it is a good moment for parents to shoulder greater ministry responsibility (which may help them to cope with the 'empty nest' syndrome).

Every member of the congregation is a minister and is equally important. There are no hierarchies. 'How important am I as compared to others in my church?' is an illegitimate question. But the pastor must help each member to find his or her appropriate role.

6. Staffing the church

What then of the paid staff of the church? If there is only one paid member of staff, it will be hard to get away from the incipient clericalism we have discussed. I think it is healthy to work towards creating a staff team as soon as possible.

However it is done, the creation of a staff team brings

potential problems as well as blessings. It is these relationships at the very heart of the local church that the devil most delights to attack. As a married minister, I must above all guard my relationship with my wife (after my relationship with Christ), but I must also guard my relationship with my closest colleagues. It is worth taking any amount of trouble over these relationships in recognition that they will attract particular Satanic attention. Loyalty begins at the point of disagreement. We have to learn to trust one another in staff teams, so that disagreements do not threaten team unity. As in marriage, it is not the eradication of conflict that we seek, but learning how to resolve conflicts so that the team effort is strengthened and not debilitated by them. That will require openness and trust.

I need to learn more and more how to draw the very best out of my colleagues by building them up, so that they grow to their full stature – and beyond it! It is said that one can only criticise a colleague effectively if one has praised him or her five times as much as one criticises. The praise creates the enlarged comfort zone in which the criticism can be accepted and, in time, acted upon. Without that affirmation the criticism may be too threatening to be incorporated into the colleague's thinking and attitudes. I need to learn to express my appreciation for my colleagues daily. Too often I take them for granted and I let my love and my thankfulness for them go unsaid.

I must learn to allow my colleagues to grow past me – indeed to train them to excel me in godliness. I have to watch out for competitiveness in the staff team – the spirit that wants to keep others down for the sake of my own security. Watch the relationships between team members' spouses as well. One pastor initiated the rule that wives interview wives before the appointment of a married man to his staff team, after someone had to leave the staff because the wives could not get on with one another.

We will want to teach our staff to lead by example – in

our deep commitment to one another, and to the gospel, and to the every member ministry of the church. For example, it is a good use of a staff member to run a crèche so that a group of young mothers can study the Bible. That exemplifies the church's priorities and it guards against staff self-importance.

7. Housing the church

In 1994 we completed a £1.8m move from one church building to another. During the transition we met for our morning services for four and a half years in the debating chamber of the Cambridge Union Society. During that time we learnt that a debating chamber is a much better place for church services than a mediaeval church building. Understanding from the New Testament why the church meets freed us from a preoccupation with buildings as a way of honouring God and concentrated our attention on making the new building user-friendly. One of the marks of a church geared to maintenance rather than growth is an obsession with church buildings and their symbolic value. God is not honoured by buildings. He is honoured by human lives offered to him in praise and service. The awe spoken of in the second half of Hebrews 12 is not the awe of tangible things that can be seen and heard (like Gothic pillars and beautiful choir music); it is awe at the gathering of the people of God in whom the Spirit of the Living God is present.

We have invested very heavily (for the first time in eight and half centuries, mind you) in a building in the hope of providing better gospel ministry in central Cambridge. It gives us a good venue for the celebration gathering of several hundred, and has enough ancillary rooms for other activities.

We are also aware that heavy investment in buildings can easily distort the life of a church, sucking money away from ministry and into plant. With a new and expensive building in our charge, it is easy for gospel priorities to get highjacked and for the tail to start wagging the dog. The uses to which

we put the building now may be a greater test of our
faithfulness than the challenge to execute the project in the
first place.

8. Funding the church

It is said to be a feature of lively, growing churches that they
lurch from one financial crisis to another. Whether we are
lively and growing or not, that certainly seems to be a feature
of St. Andrew the Great. I do not remember a time when I
have contemplated our church finances without being tempted
to anxiety. I do not have the gift of faith in this area and I am
therefore grateful to leave the financial government of the
church in the hands of those who do. (I suspect it is a wise
guideline for the pastoral leader of a local church to be
distanced from its financial administration.)

But the church finances have been our greatest spur to
prayer. There is no human logic behind them. Only miraculous
grace can explain our financial survival so far. And only
faith can face the future as we pray to God to continue to
meet our needs. I guess it is a healthy perspective. I would
not trust myself in church leadership if God replaced our
financial straits with plenty.

There is more in the New Testament about possessions
and wealth than there is about prayer. And we live in an
immensely acquisitive age. I guess this is an important area
to be teaching about in our churches. The British can be
super-spiritual about money. Wealth is a talent to be used for
the gospel just like any other talent, and those who have it
(which is most of us) will need the same teaching and
practical encouragement to put it to gospel use as we do
with our other talents. The release of funds can unlock the
administrative resources of a church to free more people for
Bible ministry. But the lack of adequate funding will
hamstring the administration of the local church and thus
curtail its Bible ministry.

It is a spiritual battle – to teach the church to give. It is done by Bible-teaching and by prayer, not by shrewd fund-raising. There is a close and complex link between prayer and the finances of a church.

9. Sending the church

I am going to draw to a close with a confession of failure: I am ashamed of what I have done to advance the cause of overseas mission at St. Andrew the Great – or rather, of what I have not done.

Cambridge has an extraordinary history of involvement with world-wide mission. We know that it is not a case of the church of God having a mission, but of the God of mission having a church. We are the only society that exists for the sake of those who are not yet its members. The church exists by mission as a fire exists by burning.

I do believe that it is the gospel that both equips for mission and motivates for mission. If God's Word is preached in all its fullness, that Word will itself drive men and women out to serve God in every continent, just as it drives them out into social and political involvement of all sorts as well. So our primary task is to keep on preaching a faithful gospel. If the congregation lacks missionary and social and political involvement, we ought to re-examine the faithfulness of the gospel we are preaching: am I teaching the whole counsel of God? I fear there is a great deal more that I could have done, particularly with the extraordinary opportunities that have opened in Eastern Europe in recent years.

10. Assessing of the church

I hope these two chapters have helped you to assess some of the weaknesses and strengths of your own church. But please remember that it is faithfulness to God's Word rather than results that is the criterion by which to judge the church. We must be obedience-orientated rather than results-orientated. Growth is God's gift to the church and not our achievement. He is answerable to no one. He retains the initiative in building his church as and where, and when, and how, he wills.

Our task remains to bring ourselves humbly and earnestly under his Word, and then to teach that Word accurately and faithfully by life and lip to those he commits to our charge. May God himself continue to empower and equip you for that work.

FAITH

Peter Jensen

9

THE NATURE OF FAITH

Peter Jensen

To the question, 'Why study Faith?' there are three answers. Firstly, such study is important because of *the significance of faith in the Bible*. A basic word study shows the vast number of instances of the word 'faith' and its cognates. For example, 'your faith has healed you' (Mark 5:34); 'believe in the Lord Jesus Christ and you will be saved' (Acts 16:31); 'I live by faith' (Gal. 2:20); 'without faith it is impossible to please God' (Heb. 11:6); 'this is the victory that has overcome the world, even our faith' (1 John 5:4).

It is not only the words for faith which show the importance of this matter. In many passages the word itself is missing, but the theme is there. In passage after passage the idea of faith and the challenge to faith are present.

Ultimately a Christian is known as a believer, and those who do not belong to Christ, whatever faith they may profess, are called unbelievers. Clearly, the bottom line is faith in Christ.

Secondly, clear thinking about faith is essential, for if we are clear on this subject *it will help us as ministers of the gospel to get our priorities right*. After all, as ministers of the gospel, our time is limited. We are always having to choose between what is urgent and what is necessary. Our main priority as preachers and teachers of the gospel is to proclaim the word which will create, encourage and strengthen faith. Thus knowledge of what faith is will help to shape our preaching. We need to have a thorough grasp of how people come to faith, and what sort of faith pleases God. We need to know what faith is if we are going to instruct and help our people.

Thirdly, clear thinking about faith will *help sort out our theological confusion.* The evangelical movement worldwide is becoming more and more confused about God, the gospel, the Scriptures and human obedience. It is frightening to see how quickly the evangelical movement has reverted to self and the experiences of self as the source of theology. Scott Hafemann, an American scholar, in commenting on this phenomenon, has said that among evangelicals 'the Bible viewed as distinct from the believer is now suspect.... "I know that Christ lives in my heart" is equated with "I know about Christ and God by looking into my heart".'[1] This is a massive shift in theological understanding.

Defining faith

One dictionary defines faith as 'confidence or trust in a person or thing'. Immediately, you will see that faith is entirely unremarkable. *Faith is a universal human experience.* Indeed it is not possible to exist in this world as a human being without faith, confidence or trust. We exercise faith continually, and at several different levels simultaneously. Faith is always relational. If this is what the author of Hebrews meant by 'faith' when he wrote, 'Without faith it is not possible to please God', then we would need have no fear, for humans are full of faith. No matter how sceptical or cynical they are, their cynicism and scepticism are far outweighed by the faith which they constantly exercise in all sorts of things and persons.

For after all, it is not faith that matters, it is faith in *what or whom.* We don't pride ourselves on having faith, so unremarkable and constant is it. Therefore, when people say to you, as they sometimes do, 'I cannot find faith' or 'I admire you because you have faith' or something similar, they don't actually mean that they cannot exercise faith, for indeed they exercise it constantly and simultaneously at various levels. To them the meaning of faith is determined by the object of faith. It is this that makes faith useful or dangerous, saving or not. There are two points about saving faith that I wish to make at this stage.

Firstly, *saving faith comes from the gospel and focuses on Christ*. Faith is spoken of in the New Testament overwhelmingly as faith in Jesus Christ. Although there are times when it speaks about faith in God, again and again the central business of the New Testament is faith in Jesus Christ. Christian faith is unambiguously, unremittingly, Christ-centred. It is when Christ is preached that faith comes into existence. The gospel is not about faith, the gospel is about Jesus Christ. Faith springs into existence as people learn to trust him and to give their lives to him. Christian faith is nothing else than faith in Jesus Christ as he is presented to us in the Word of God.

If you wish to sum up in two or three words the whole message of the Word of God, it is this: Jesus Christ is Lord. Therefore, when the message of Jesus Christ the Lord is preached, men and women exercise a *repentant* faith. The first and most wonderful fruit of faith is always repentance, as men and women turn from the idols in which they trusted and commit themselves into the hands of the Lord Jesus Christ. Faith and repentance are really two aspects of the same thing, for Christian faith is trust in the Lord Jesus Christ as he is presented to us in the Scriptures. The gospel also persuades us of the truth about Jesus, and faith responds to the gospel with both the assent of the mind and the trust of the heart. The Bible speaks of its great heroes as 'full of faith', but the point is not that they are full of faith, but that they are full of faith in the Saviour. Faith takes its strength and its shape and its purpose from the gospel of the Lord Jesus.

Secondly, *saving faith is the gift of God's Spirit*. Sinful and rebellious people are utterly incapable of responding to God. Paul in 2 Corinthians 4:3-4 indicates this incapacity:

And even if our gospel is veiled, it is veiled to those who are perishing. The god of this age has blinded the minds of unbelievers, so that they cannot see the light of the gospel of the glory of Christ, who is the image of God.

In those few pithy words, Paul sets out the terrible plight of the human race, unable to respond to the gospel. The evil one has blinded the minds of unbelievers so they cannot see the light of the gospel of the glory of Christ. Paul goes right back to the tremendous work of God in creation, when God told light to shine in the darkness, in order to illustrate the illumination God gives to blinded sinners. The gospel can be accepted only when God illuminates the minds of unbelievers by his Holy Spirit.

In 1 Corinthians 2:4, 5, Paul writes: 'My message and my preaching were not with wise and persuasive words, but with a demonstration of the Spirit's power, so that your faith might not rest on men's wisdom, but on God's power.' In 1 Thessalonians 1:5, Paul speaks of the power of the Spirit of God. In 1 Thessalonians 2:13, he speaks of the power of the Word of God. Word and Spirit belong together, they must never be separated. It is by the power of the Spirit of God taking the Word of God and illuminating our hearts that we come to know God. When we are asked where saving faith comes from, the answer is that it comes through the preaching of the gospel blessed by the Spirit of God.

God is entirely sovereign, both in accomplishing and applying redemption. Although there is the human effort of preaching the gospel, although it is perfectly true that faith is a human activity, in the final analysis no-one ever comes to faith in Christ except by the powerful work of the Spirit of God in drawing and bringing that person. Preachers do not have to find faith lurking in the hearts of their listeners, preachers do not have to engender faith. Their business is the ministry of the Word of God and prayer. The Word of God itself will draw forth faith when blessed by the Spirit of God. Saving faith is created by the Word and the Spirit. Although God has used human individuals to bring most of his people to faith in him, yet the work that ministers of the gospel do is nothing, for it is God's work that brings faith.

John Calvin's definition of faith can hardly be surpassed as a summary teaching on New Testament faith: 'a firm and certain knowledge of God's benevolence of us, founded upon the truth of the freely given promise in Christ, both revealed to our minds and sealed on our hearts through the Holy Spirit.'[2] That is faith.

Faith and superstition

My dictionary, however, gave a second definition of faith: it is 'belief which is not based on truth'. Some people put their faith in a rabbit's foot or a St. Christopher medal. How do you tell the difference between faith in a rabbit's foot and faith in Jesus Christ? As remarked on already, it is not the faith itself, but the object of faith, that gives it its shape and purpose and strength. It's best then to use the word *superstition* for faith in the wrong object. Superstition is faith gone wrong; it is faith, but faith in an error. Superstition can be tremendously strong: you can have an extraordinarily strong faith in your lucky number. In fact sometimes some people's superstitious faith is so strong it can almost seem to create its own success. But full faith in a lie is much worse than little faith in the truth. In the end it matters very little whether we have small faith or struggling faith or inadequate faith as long as it is faith in the truth, for by attaching ourselves to the truth the power of faith comes true.

Superstition was a great Reformation category. The Reformers, in their day, had to break their way through a thicket of superstition that had gripped the Church. We have forgotten many of the great truths of the Reformation and, as a result, superstition is creeping back into the churches with no-one to say it nay.

It is interesting to note that today the Reformers are often regarded as fools and bigots by the world and in the church. But they were prepared to be negative, to label error as error.

They were prepared to change the church furniture, and to change the architecture to make it reflect the gospel of the Lord Jesus Christ. Since the middle of the nineteenth century, the Anglican Church has been changing the furniture back to reflect superstition. Reformers were burnt in the sixteenth century; in the twentieth century their reputations have been scorched too, because people are unprepared to see that faith depends upon truth and that we must stand for the truth.

For we have faith in the faith. The New Testament not only speaks of faith meaning our inward attitude to Christ, but it also speaks of *the* faith, and that quite frequently. For example, in Jude verse 3, Christians are called upon to contend for the faith that was once for all entrusted to the saints. The faith is encapsulated in the Word of God, the Scriptures, and we are told by Jesus that man does not live by bread alone but on every word that comes from the mouth of God (Matt. 4:4). Therefore, when you trust in the gospel of the Lord Jesus you inevitably trust in the Scriptures which incorporate that gospel.

There are great dangers to the faith these days, and hence great dangers to Christian obedience. When the Word of God is subverted, when the truth is undermined, faith will necessarily suffer and so will worship and all Christian obedience – for our faith is based upon the truth. The key point of the assault against Christianity will always be the assault upon the Word of God. Scepticism comes with all the regalia of academic success. Many are unprepared to say that the Scriptures are the Word of God and they accuse those who do of bibliolatry.

Many churches today teach that God speaks in other ways apart from his Word. Listening to God involves interpreting dreams, visions, experiences and prophecies. All sorts of things are coming in as a word of God, and we are being asked to trust in them rather than the Scriptures. Those who follow this teaching are mingling faith with superstition.

The evangelical faith is often criticized for being very

cerebral. But believing in the gospel is the most blessed and wonderful experience. There is no experience like the experience of being found by God, of having his light illuminate our minds so that we may see the glory of God in the face of our wonderful and blessed Saviour, Jesus Christ. What experience compares to that? Is it against the truth? No, it is the truth. Does it bypass the mind? No, it captures the mind.

Of course, there are other experiences of God. We are aware of the beauty of nature and we stand in awe of God's marvellous and wonderful creative power. We sometimes wonder at answers to our prayers or are astonished by what God does. There are times when our hearts burst with love in the presence of God. Sometimes experiences confirm and strengthen the faith of those who already believe.

Sometimes, however, our experiences contradict faith. What happens when what we have been praying for does not happen? Many, who continually refer to their experiences, only talk about positive experiences. But Christian experience is far wider than that. Our prayers may not be answered as we want, we can fall into danger and despair, our spiritual life may be narrowed. In such times we have to walk by faith. It is not faith in experiences that is needed but faith in Jesus.

If faith is as I have described it, then the continuous exposition of the Scriptures is the chief function of ministers of the gospel, and the proclamation of the Scriptures and their application is our chief business in every situation. If faith is as I have described it, then the groups that are associated with our churches will not be counselling groups or therapy groups. Instead faithful, obedient people will make up Bible study groups and groups meeting for prayer. The Christian life is founded on the truth of God's revealed Word. If we falter here we will produce religious people, but not Christians.

Notes
1. 'Seminary, Subjectivity, and the Centrality of Scripture: Reflections on the current Crisis in Evangelical Seminary Education' in *Journal of the Evangelical Theological Society* 31, 2 (1988) p.136.

2. J.T. McNeill (ed), F.L. Battles (trans), John Calvin, *Institutes of the Christian Religion* (Book 3, chapter 2, section 7), (Westminster: Philadelphia, 1960), p.551.

10

THE ASSURANCE OF FAITH

Peter Jensen

Doubtless in your experience of Christian ministry, as in mine, there have been various defining moments. For me, one of those moments was a conversation that I had with a young student who was attending my church. I can remember sitting on the front steps of the church chatting to her about her problem of doubt. In trying to discover her particular difficulty I mentioned to her several causes of doubt, such as the miracles of the Bible or whether or not other religions will save people, or the problem of suffering. But to all these suggestions she answered 'No'. Her doubt was whether God would accept her. Although she was a Christian, she was deeply concerned about her acceptability to God; she was in despair about it. I myself had been troubled with intellectual doubts, but the question of whether or not God would accept me hardly crossed my mind. I realized then that there were people who had different doubts. My question at that stage in my life was, 'Where is the true God?' But her question was, 'Where is the gracious God?' In her experience of the Christian life she was conscious of sin, she was conscious of guilt, she was aware of the judgment that lay ahead. And she had responded to her doubt with attempts to be good.

If you have been in Christian ministry for any length of time, you will know that plenty of people are in exactly that situation. Their consciences are very tender and sensitive, therefore their joy flickers on and off. They feel themselves to be failures as Christians. Although they know that they belong to the Lord Jesus, they worry about their continued acceptability to him. A Christian psychologist once said to

me: 'In your preaching, you certainly afflict the comfortable.
But I wish you would also comfort the afflicted as well, for
after you preach the queues outside my room on Monday
mornings are doubled.' The fact of the matter is that many of
our people are indeed the afflicted.

Today, through the impact of post-modernity, there is a
new focus. It's not as though the intellectual problems have
disappeared or that the problems of guilt and sin have gone
away. But the focus has shifted, and Christians now sense
they are weak, vulnerable and powerless. They are being
asked to hold on to a faith that the vast majority do not have.
The question today is not so much, 'Where is the true God?',
or even, 'Where is the gracious God?', but, 'Where is the
living God?'

I suspect many believers have this problem. But I would
say that it is those who minister the Word of God and their
wives who are most conscious of the weakness of the church,
of the powerlessness of the Christian, and who know
something of the despair of being in an institution in decline.
From their hearts comes the cry, 'Where is the living God?'
To minister for years in a small congregation and to see
nothing happening, makes one ask, 'Where is the living God?'
Such people ask God to give them an experience which will
confirm their faith, which will give them power, which will
make them bold, which will, as some say, release the Spirit's
energy into the world.

The search for divine assurance
For over a hundred years now, through books and
conferences, one suggested answer is that by following
certain rules or taking certain steps, our weakness can become
power. We have become involved in what I call the quest
for assurance.

Of course, some observers do not have my view of the
way things are in the churches. They are buoyant and
optimistic about the state of Christianity and would point, as

evidence for their optimism, to the renewal of Christian music and to the mega-conventions. To my mind, however, as I try to analyse what is going on, it seems that a lot of the excitement has to do, not so much with the idea that God's great power is being released in the world, but rather with a quest for personal assurance. What we are seeing is not a huge outburst of spiritual energy and revival throughout the world, but a renewal of confidence that God does love 'me' despite the experiences 'I' have had. People are looking for their weak faith to change to an assured confidence that God does love them, longing for the boldness and freedom that will bring. But are they looking in the right place?

In the seventeenth century in England, there developed amongst English-speaking Christians a distinction between Christian faith and Christian assurance. It was understood that saving faith need only be a mustard seed of faith in order to be saving. But it was also suggested that between such a saving faith and assurance there could exist a gap, perhaps of some years. It followed from this that the Christian life was largely made up of the move from faith in God to assurance that God was indeed the gracious and accepting God. So, for many, the Christian life became a quest for assurance.

The reality of one's faith could be shown by keeping God's Word. A person could demonstrate the reality of faith and therefore possess assurance as long as he was obedient to the Lord. So the move from faith to assurance ran along the path of the good works which demonstrated the reality of one's faith. This idea was strangely parallel to, although not the same as, the Roman Catholic belief of salvation by God's grace and human good works. And interestingly there was a substantial interest in those days in Catholic devotional literature to help people move from faith to assurance. True, they removed the references to the Mass and other obvious blemishes, but the heart of this devotional literature remained. In particular, there was an interest in the various techniques that people could use. One example was meditation by which a person, when reading about the life of Jesus, could, by so concentrating on the life of Jesus, move his affections on to the next stage and release himself for various good works.

This type of Christian literature resulted in an impressive flowering of devotion that was extraordinarily legalistic and burdensome. But it was not a growth in the understanding of the Christian faith. Instead it was a shift away from the Reformed doctrines which had cleared away such burdensome things and left individuals face to face with the law of God in all its strength and power. In this new movement the law of God was being continually split up into tiny parts, so that people could keep this element or that element. Why was it necessary to do that?

The answer is that any system which incorporates human obedience as a necessary element will fail to reassure. It may give assurance for a little while, but the more human elements there are in any system, the more sensitive consciences will recognize that even the smallest amount of human effort is flawed by sin. Assurance can never be gained by such efforts. They will lead either to Pharisaism, in which people think they actually have obeyed the law, or to despair even more profound than that with which they started.

I was interested in the light of this to read a reflective book called *Charismatic Renewal* by Tom Smail, Andrew Walker and Nigel Wright who I understand have all been touched by the renewal. Nigel Wright tells how, during his university years, he was challenged by some who had already entered into the experience, and he discovered the gift of tongues. Wright's comment on what had happened is significant: 'On reflection I see that this experience had more to do with assurance of salvation than with spiritual power.' I think he is absolutely right. The charismatic blessing which he is talking about is only one of a number of possible routes to reassurance. Wright goes on:

I am of the opinion that the experiences which are often called Baptism of the Spirit might properly be understood within the context of the doctrine of assurance. They are heart warming moments when the knowledge of salvation wells up within the heart. To know that I too was not excluded from God's grace but made its object, did a lot for me, giving me a spiritual importance which was to lead me to a vocation in the ministry on completing university.[1]

Wright has pin-pointed what seems to be happening in so many lives. People may tell us that they are looking for power to serve Christ, but the underlying issue is a matter of assurance. However, that leads us to ask if they have understood assurance properly.

The experience-based assurance of today has these features.

(1) It is understood as confidence before God and power before the world.

(2) It is gained through the taking of special steps, perhaps a prayer, a discipline that one enters, a meeting that one attends, a technique that one employs.

(3) It is experienced in a direct touch from God, a dream perhaps, an ecstasy, a speaking in tongues, a miracle, an exaltation, some special touch from God, reassuring the person that there is a living God and that he is loved by this living God.

(4) It is exemplified in Christian leadership through books, videos, television programmes and through personal ministry by the leader.

(5) It is very anecdotal.

(6) It results in boldness, enthusiasm, love for Christ, obedience, scripture reading and prayer. Often it has great results in the life of the person who seeks for an experience-based assurance.

Let me make some theological comments on this quest.

First, *the quest for assurance, as I understand it, is*

thoroughly legitimate. Christians should be joyful and have a confidence in their standing before God.

Secondly, *the method stems from a valid insight.* We can become more conscious of the love of God from Christian experience. For example, an answer to prayer, the experience of the love of the brethren, a spiritual high point, and so on, come frequently enough for us to have learned that we can draw great consolation and comfort from them.

Thirdly, although the quest itself is legitimate, some words of caution are needed. *The need for experience-based assurance can divert attention from Christ to ourselves*, to techniques, to gurus, to introspection.

Fourthly, *it underestimates human sinfulness* by suggesting that we can secure the Lord's response through the steps which we take. Whenever human effort is given a key role, it fails. However much we put into the effort, it is never good enough and it leads to either despair or hypocrisy.

After I was converted, I read the books of Watchman Nee, and other similar authors. Their books informed me that if I followed a particular technique, I could have the victory over sin. I actually experienced a kind of 'second blessing'. For the next three years I worked hard for the promised victory, but to no avail.

The problem is that this type of teaching underestimates the sinfulness of sin. Also it reduces God's sovereignty to the strange and the bizarre and the striking. It locates God in dreams and tongues and miracles, but it doesn't locate him in the ordinary, in Bible study for example. In doing so, it unintentionally reduces the sovereignty of God so that he becomes a God of the spectacular gaps. It fails to see that all such spiritual experiences are human as much as they are divine. For these things happen to non-Christians as well as to Christians. Therefore they cannot be said to show that God loves 'me'.

What of the fact that many people are blessed through such experiences? Do we need to deny that they are blessed?

No. I was blessed through my experience of the second blessing. But in the end it took me years to work it through and to put it behind me. Although there were many ill features of it, there were blessings in it as well. For example, it was after I had received the blessing that the Lord first used me to lead a person to him. And there are many who will testify to the way in which such experiences have unlocked spiritual blessings in various ways.

The recent Toronto Blessing appears to me to have been ridiculous. I was saddened to see the Christian church diverted into something that seemed so ludicrous. Yet what are we to make of the fact that many were blessed through it, that it watered the dry ground of their spiritual life, and that it caused them to read their Bibles more, to pray more, to witness more? It would be foolish to say those benefits did not happen. But we need to observe that non-Christians had the experience too. The phenomenon was not uniquely Christian, it was really a human phenomenon which occurred within a Christian context. Undoubtedly, many have taken it to be the strengthening hand of God upon their lives. When faith is strengthened, then of course good things happen. But, overall we may still come to view the effects of such teaching as unwholesome and not useful, just as were the effects of the teaching I received from writers like Watchman Nee.

The Toronto Blessing will be replaced by something else in a few years' time. In the 1980s, it was signs and wonders; in 1991 it was prophecy; in 1995 it was the Toronto Blessing. The reason is that experience-based assurance can never ultimately satisfy. For that is not the way in which true assurance comes.

True assurance
So where may we find true assurance of faith? In 1979 Billy Graham was interviewed on television in Sydney. The interviewer asked Dr. Graham, 'Do you believe that you are going to heaven when you die?' Billy replied, 'Yes.' That

conversation jammed the switchboard, prompting more angry calls than anything prior to it. Most people believe that we cannot say *we are* going to heaven through our good works and experience, for our good works are never good enough. The most that they are prepared to say is, 'I *believe* that I am going to heaven when I die.' When they heard Billy Graham say he *knows* that he is going to heaven when he dies, they assumed his assurance was there because he had preached to millions of people and had been the advisor to presidents and so on. In other words, they thought he was proud and full of himself. But Billy Graham's assurance was based on the Word of God, on what it teaches regarding salvation from sin through faith in Christ.

That is assurance; it is based not on some word from within ourselves, but on the word of the gospel which comes from outside us and speaks so powerfully of what Jesus has done.

Such assurance assumes *the grace of God*. On the other hand, experiential assurance finds something in us, be it a moral success perhaps, or a second blessing, or a path of spirituality. Whatever it is, it is an event that has occurred to us, and experiential assurance uses it as the ground for deducing that God does love us after all. But the Word of God assumes our total incapacity, our total depravity. The Bible emphasizes the verdict of God that we are totally corrupt and unable to please him. It is only when we realize our complete lack of any capacity to please God, even as Christians, that we find true assurance by clinging to the cross. The gospel of the Lord Jesus Christ says that the ground of our assurance is our *justification*.

In Romans 5:1, Paul writes that 'since we have been justified through faith, we have peace with God through our Lord Jesus Christ'. Faith in Jesus Christ has given us access 'into this grace in which we now stand'. We do not stand in any experience which we have had, we do not stand in any progress we have made, we do not stand in our success in the battle against sin – we stand in the grace of the Lord Jesus Christ by which he has justified us.

So, despite adverse circumstances, 'we also rejoice in our sufferings, because we know that suffering produces perseverance; perseverance, character; and character, hope. And hope does not disappoint us, because God has poured out his love into our hearts by the Holy Spirit, whom he has given us' (Rom. 5:3-5). It is possible for us to read this as meaning that God has given us love in our hearts, that is, the capacity to love others. But that is wrong. This text is saying that it is the ministry of the Holy Spirit in our hearts which convinces us of the love of God for us.

I think a number of translations are wrong to begin a new paragraph after verse 5. Verses 6-8 describe how the Holy Spirit convinces us of the love of God for us:

> You see, at just the right time, when we were still powerless, Christ died for the ungodly. Very rarely will anyone die for a righteous man, though for a good man someone might possibly dare to die. But God demonstrates his own love for us in this: While we were still sinners, Christ died for us.

The ground of our assurance is the grace of God expressed in the love of Christ in his death for us on the cross. To weak, foolish, helpless and incapable sinners, that is Christian assurance, for it does not rely on us at all but on the great power of God. Christian assurance turns again and again to the story of the cross of Christ. Believers never graduate beyond the cross, they are always returning to it and take their stand there.

When we have received this assurance of the love of God through the cross of Christ, not based on anything in ourselves but on what God has done for us in Christ, then we understand the world for what it is and we can trust in the *sovereignty* of our Father.

And we know that in all things God works for the good of those who love him, who have been called according to his purpose. For those God foreknew he also predestined to be conformed to the likeness of his Son, that he might be the firstborn among many brothers. And those he predestined, he also called; those he called, he also justified; those he justified, he also glorified (Rom. 8:28-30).

We who belong to the Lord Jesus; we who by the ministry of the Holy Spirit in our hearts focusing us again and again on the cross, are assured of the love of God towards us. We may say that the good things and the bad things, the extraordinary answers to prayer and the deep sufferings, all work together for our good. But we need to understand the word *good*. In the context, the good is to become like Jesus. Those who cling to the cross have such a view of the sovereignty of God that suffering itself is our servant. Sadly, faith based on experience will never be rugged enough to cope with that. It will always be looking for the next experience to refresh and revive. But faith based on the cross will never weary, for the cross never changes. Such assurance is not based on our capacity or our experiences, but simply on what God has done *for* us and what he *is* now doing in us.

Paul asks the question: 'Who will separate us from the love of Christ?' (Rom. 8:35). In his answer he says, 'No, in all these things we are more than conquerors through him who *loved* us' (verse 37). If you had been writing that verse you would never have written what Paul wrote. Under the influence of the modern church's teaching, you would have said, 'In all these things we are more than conquerors through him who *loves* us.' That is what people want; to know that God does love them despite everything.

Why did Paul use the past tense? Because he could never get away from the cross. Of course, he knew himself to be the object of the on-going, unceasing, sustaining love of God. But he understood that if he wished to be reassured, he would

have to go back to the cross. It's on the basis of that cross
that he then goes on to write:

> For I am convinced that neither death nor life, neither angels
> nor demons, neither the present nor the future, nor any powers,
> neither height nor depth, nor anything else in all creation, will
> be able to separate us from the love of God that is in Christ
> Jesus our Lord (Rom. 8: 38-39).

Faith is amazing! Faith is wonderful, not because it is
anything in itself, but because it is faith in Jesus, and it brings
us into touch with Jesus.

How should I have helped the student who came to me
with her problem of doubt? I could have said to her: 'You
are simply not old enough to have committed the really big
sins. The sins that are weighing on your conscience are just
not big enough for God to be angry with.' If I had given her
that advice, it would not have been at all helpful.

Or I could have said to her: 'I'm glad you mentioned this
because I had exactly the same problem when I was a
teenager. And I found that by praying for a special blessing
of the Holy Spirit, along with complete repentance and
absolute faith, I found the victory life pouring forth.' She
could have had an experience right then and it may have
been great for a while.

But what I would have to say to her is this: 'Your
conscience is telling you the truth when it points out your sin
to you. But it is not telling you *the whole truth*. If only you
knew what you look like to God, you would be really
horrified. Yes, you are a sinful person and the only hope for
you is the grace of God expressed in the cross of Christ. It is
there that you will find the peace of God.'

Where is the living God? Why, he is exactly where he has
always been – in the gospel. The modern church seems to
have lost confidence in the gospel. It allows that we can
start with the gospel but then we have to go on to something

else. But the living God is in the gospel. We will do well to
cling to the cross, to minister the gospel of the love of God
in Jesus Christ who died on the cross. We will do well to
preach that gospel with all its ramifications, not holding back
on sin and its sinfulness, but making sure we exalt the Saviour.
If we do so, our people will rejoice every day in the living
God who is Jesus Christ our Lord.

Notes

1. T. Small, A Walker, N. Wright, *Charismatic Renewal*, SPCK.

11

THE LIFE OF FAITH

Peter Jensen

How do we live by faith? For the preacher this question is even more complex: 'How can I challenge my people to live by faith when I live by faith inadequately myself?'

There are two passages in Scripture that speak particularly of the life of faith. The first of these states:

> I have been crucified with Christ and I no longer live, but Christ lives in me. The life I live in the body, I live by faith in the Son of God, who loved me and gave himself for me (Gal. 2:20).

The second passage concludes:

> Therefore we are always confident and know that as long as we are at home in the body we are away from the Lord. We live by faith, not by sight. We are confident, I say, and would prefer to be away from the body and at home with the Lord. So we make it our goal to please him, whether we are at home in the body or away from it. For we must all appear before the judgment seat of Christ, that each one may receive what is due to him for the things done while in the body, whether good or bad (2 Cor. 5:6-10).

There are some very helpful points to make from these passages.

Firstly, when Paul says that believers live by faith he does not mean that they live without any visible means of financial support. In actual fact, the life of faith does not refer to something special or saintly, attained by only the few, a higher victory life – it means simply the Christian life. A Christian person lives by faith because his faith is focused in the Son of God; the Christian life is the life of faith in the Son of God. Christian faith is well and truly tethered and secured to Jesus Christ, to the Son of God who loved me and gave himself for me.

I don't think that there is a more glorious description of Christian faith in the whole of the Bible. Paul shows us that Christian faith takes its roots and its meaning and its shape from an object, namely – Jesus Christ.

In 2 Corinthians 5:7, faith is contrasted with sight, with our final experience. But believers aim to please the Lord while they are waiting for sight. In other words faith lives the Christian life, and that life will be tested when they stand before the judgment seat of Christ.

Why do you think God chose faith as the salvation point? Why did he not choose love? Because faith is the very opposite of pride and exaltation and glory. If he had said love, then there would have been something in us that would have made us worthy of salvation. Faith is the empty hand grasping hold of the promises of God. It has no power until it is itself attached to God's power.

In Matthew 17:20 the Lord Jesus says: 'I tell you the truth, if you have faith as small as a mustard seed, you can say to this mountain, "Move from here to there" and it will move. Nothing will be impossible for you.' What did Jesus mean when he said that faith could move mountains? He meant that God provides the power when faith attaches itself to him. There are many mighty works of faith revealed in the Bible, and I want to look at three of them in particular.

We read in Romans 5:1: 'Therefore, since we have been justified through faith we have peace with God.' Perhaps you do not think justification is as impressive as resurrecting someone from the dead or moving a mountain. However, I think that moving the mountain of our sin was a fairly significant thing for faith to accomplish.

We were legally condemned for our sins. Not even repentance can wipe away the sins of the past. Not even a life filled with the good works of Florence Nightingale would make the slightest bit of difference to the adverse judgment against us. Because of what we have done we are indeed the fitting subjects of the wrath of God. In Exodus 23:7, it says that 'God never acquits the guilty'. But in Romans 4:5 Paul says that God 'justifies the ungodly'. In between those two statements there lies the cross to make them both true.

What power faith has that we may be justified, that forgiveness may come into lives that are corrupt, ignorant of God and rebellious against him! Some people think that God gave us the Ten Commandments so that we could be saved by keeping them. But when that didn't work, God sent Jesus and all we have to do now is have faith. In this view, faith is a substitute for obedience. But justification has always been through faith in Jesus Christ. It was so for Abraham as well as for Paul and Peter. Faith is the cry to God from the despairing heart, it is the response to Jesus' invitation to the weak and heavy laden to come to him. How powerful faith is that it can bring justification to the ungodly!

Faith: the power to sustain the Christian

The Christian life begins with faith in Christ and it goes on by faith in Christ. It is not as though we begin as sinful people but are turned suddenly into sinless people who no longer need the cross. On the contrary, the more we go on in the Christian life, the more we become aware of the depths of sin, of the sinfulness of our hearts. As we go on in the Christian life, the Son of God appears more and more glorious in all his saving power through the cross. We become more and more grateful to the grace of God displayed at the cross of Christ. We can never graduate beyond this point because faith in Christ always takes us to Christ and to the cross of Christ. Our life is a life of walking by faith.

It is that faith that we read about in Hebrews 11. Undoubtedly those early heroes of the faith had only the scantiest information about what God was going to do. But

the word of God which came to them, to Noah, to Abraham,
to Moses, was a word of promise. It pointed forward to the
Lord Jesus Christ. So their faith was exactly the same as
ours – it was faith in that word that pointed them to the Lord
Jesus Christ.

Notice that the great heroes of faith had very different
circumstances. Some lived in easier times than others,
although most had their difficulties. Some knew triumph, such
as Noah who was vindicated in this life. But others
experienced apparent defeat, where there was no vindication
in this life:

> They were stoned; they were sawn in two; they were put to
> death by the sword. They went about in sheepskins and
> goatskins, destitute, persecuted and ill-treated – the world was
> not worthy of them. They wandered in deserts and mountains,
> and in caves and holes in the ground (Heb. 11:37-38).

But what we see in all cases is faith in the word of God and
triumphing in that.

We could not judge from their outward circumstances
whether or not God was with them, just as we cannot judge
from personal circumstances whether a person is a great
person of faith. For faith is a hidden, private, invisible thing.
What we do see is a consistent, steady, powerful trust in
God in all circumstances.

What of us? The writer continues in Hebrews 12:1-6:

> Therefore, since we are surrounded by such a great cloud of
> witnesses, let us throw off everything that hinders and the sin
> that so easily entangles, and let us run with perseverance the
> race marked out for us. Let us fix our eyes on Jesus, the author
> and perfector of our faith, who for the joy set before him
> endured the cross, scorning its shame, and sat down at the
> right hand of the throne of God. Consider him who endured
> such opposition from sinful men, so that you will not grow
> weary and lose heart.

In your struggle against sin, you have not yet resisted to the point of shedding your blood. And you have forgotten that word of encouragement that addresses you as sons: 'My son, do not make light of the Lord's discipline, and do not lose heart when he rebukes you, because the Lord disciplines those he loves, and he punishes everyone he accepts as a son...'

What a marvellous picture of the life of faith: fixing your eyes upon Jesus, struggling against sin, being aware of the Lord's discipline, enduring suffering and pain and inconvenience. Faith introduces us to our heavenly and sovereign Father who is in charge of our lives. If Jesus Christ is our Lord, then we may be sure that the sovereign hand of God is upon our lives and that he is towards us as Father not as judge. When faith is sealed in our hearts by the Holy Spirit, we see God in all his fatherly goodness beaming upon us, and even though the circumstances in our lives may be extremely rugged and even involve the disciplining hand of God upon us, yet none the less by faith we know that all things work together for our good.

So we have seen two of the Bible's teachings on faith: it has the power to justify, and it has the power to sustain the Christian life.

Faith: the power to produce obedience

As mentioned earlier, Paul points out that all Christians are to walk by faith and not by sight, and are to make it their goal to please him. There are five points to note about obedience.

First, *by faith we receive the Holy Spirit* who enables us to obey. As we put our faith in Jesus, so we receive the Holy Spirit and the Spirit within us brings forth the fruit of obedience.

Secondly, because we have been justified, *we are free to do good works for the right reason*. We obey simply because the Lord has asked us to do so and we wish to please him who has done so much for us. Out of the faith that justifies emerges a tremendous explosion of obedience. This obedience is a recognition of grace and all that God has done for us. True obedience to God can only come through justification by faith. If we cease to preach the grace of God through justification we will cut off the roots of obedience. There will be no true worship of God and living for God if people do not understand the grace of God in justification

Thirdly, *by faith we are prepared to trust and to do the commands of God that to the world are ridiculous*. Have you ever thought about how strange it is to love enemies? Such behaviour is unusual, even ridiculous, unless we have faith in the word of him who tells us to do it. Then we are free and released to do what seems so foolish. God sometimes does give us what, humanly speaking, may seem like ridiculous commands to obey. Only by trusting God will we do what he says.

Fourthly, *by faith we are led by the Spirit's Word, the Bible*. Living by faith does not mean always living without support, although sometimes it may. I am not denying the great stories of faith where Christians have had their needs supplied from no obvious human source. But if you think that is what the life of faith is, then it will lead in the end to superstition. The Scriptures tell us to work for our living, although there may be certain circumstances where God will bring about great blessing in ways that are unexpected.

Fifthly, *by faith we will live without religiosity before God*. Matthew 6 describes how faith gives in secret, faith fasts in secret, faith prays in secret. Religiosity, which we see all around us, is created by lack of assurance. Religiosity is the religion that whispers in our ear again and again that God can't really do this, that we have to do it. Religiosity brings the law of God down to our size and makes up for it in fussy enthusiasm, with extraordinary church services, with wonderful clothes and all that sort of nonsense. Religiosity makes up for the lack of obedience to the Word of God.

By faith we can look at God's law and not quail or step

back. We can look in awe, without the need to reduce the law of God to our own size as the merely religious do. By faith we seek to obey God's law directly and faithfully. When failure occurs, as it will often do, it will not lead to despair or cover up; faith will lead us back to the cross and to grace and to repentance. Thus faith in the gospel creates a godliness which is invisible but genuine. A genuine evangelical godliness is not boastful, is not showy, it thinks much about fearing the Lord and serving the Lord rather than the development of the self.

The power of faith is not seen in spectacular healing miracles or in getting people to laugh or make animal noises. We see the power of faith in an honest Christian business man or woman. We see the power of faith in a pastor who prays in secret.

How much faith do we need?

The New Testament tells us that Stephen and Barnabas were full of faith. It is true to say that we all ought to be full of faith, for it is sinful of us to doubt God's Word. We ought to be full of faith in the Word of God. If we wish to grow in faith, if we wish to see others grow in faith, it must be through the preaching of the Word of God. Faith also grows; as we experience God's goodness our faith grows, but it is all controlled and sourced by the Word of God itself and prayer.

Actually faith doesn't give much attention to faith. Faith gives attention to Jesus. Therefore, if it is your wish to grow in faith, then grow in your knowledge of Jesus and he will call forth that faith by which you should live.

In conclusion, I would make two points. First, large faith, if it is resting in nonsense, is quite useless or even dangerous. Secondly, small faith in the truth brings great blessing. In Luke 17:5-6, when the disciples said to Jesus, 'Lord, increase our faith', did he instantly send them to the bookstall to find books on the techniques of living the Christian life? Did he send them away for a week's silence? No, he said, 'If you have faith as small as a mustard seed, you can say to this mulberry tree, "Be uprooted and planted in the sea," and it will obey you.' What an extraordinary answer. Small faith in the truth brings great blessing. It is not the size of our faith that matters in the end, it is the size of our God that matters.

A little faith in a great God is enough to bring great power, even the power of salvation. Your justification, your sustaining day by day, the power of obedience, these are the great works of God in our midst. This is the life of faith. God be praised that the work of faith is going on magnificently. God is moving mountains every day and we rejoice at the great things he has done.

12

A CHURCH FOR
THE 21ST CENTURY?

David Jackman

A CHURCH FOR THE 21ST CENTURY?

David Jackman

It is not my intention to try to read the next century, or even the next decade, with predictions as to what shape the church might be. I am neither a prophet, nor the son of a prophet. There are plenty of prognostications currently, and I imagine that they will only multiply as the century draws to its close. But I do think there is real value in taking our bearings, as evangelical ministers, and trying to work out exactly where we are, so that we can discuss and pray about what we need to do together, in order to be the faithful people of God, at this particular point in history, and in our particular part of the world. There is no doubt that by all the outward markers, we are still in a period of considerable decline. It is encouraging to know that the evangelical churches appear to be holding their own against the massive erosion that is still happening all around us, but all the surveys show that the only religious group that is constantly increasing, in our culture, is the 'no religion' group. As Phillip Jensen has commented in his characteristically pithy way, 'They are the only ones that have no nominals!' While the religious surveys still produce percentages up to approximately 75% affirming that the general public still believe in God, it is painfully obvious that God's word is still wilfully and persistently rejected by our society as a whole.

However, we need to read beyond the statistics and the projections of the pundits to the end of the story.

'Then I heard what sounded like a great multitude, like the roar of rushing waters and like loud peals of thunder, shouting:

"Hallelujah!
   For our Lord God Almighty reigns.
Let us rejoice and be glad
   and give him glory!
For the wedding of the Lamb has come,
   and his bride has made herself ready.
Fine linen, bright and clean,
   was given her to wear."
(Fine linen stands for the righteous acts of the saints.)

Then the angel said to me, "Write: Blessed are those who are invited to the wedding supper of the Lamb!" And he added, "These are the true words of God" ' (Rev. 19:6-9).

There will be a bride; there will be a wedding feast. 'These are the true words of God.' So, this must always be the ultimate perspective we have to bring to bear on the present and on the future, both immediate and eternal. This is cause enough for us to be optimists; to go on, not irrationally but faithfully, believing that God is drawing a great multitude of people to himself, and that they will be innumerable on the last day. We do not know how it will work out and we cannot foresee the game plan. But we do know what the outcome will be. The result is absolutely certain, so we can be confident in playing out our part in the light of God's unquestionable fulfilment of all his promises to Abraham and all who are his offspring, through faith in our Lord Jesus Christ. Because the wedding supper is the end point, the creation and continued existence of the bride is clearly the present strategy.

'I saw the Holy City, the new Jerusalem, coming down out of heaven from God, prepared as a bride beautifully dressed for her husband. And I heard a loud voice from the throne saying, "Now the dwelling of God is with men, and he will live with them. They will be his people, and God himself will be with them and be their God" ' (Rev. 21:2-3).

The church, then, is the focus of God's eternal plan. At last year's EMA, we studied Ephesians, and were reminded that 'God's intention is that now, through the church, the manifold wisdom of God should be made known to the rulers and authorities in the heavenly realms, according to his eternal purpose which he accomplished in Christ Jesus our Lord' (Eph. 3:10-11). God's *eternal* purpose is seen *now* in the church, growing up into him who is the head, that is Christ. The health and vitality of the church is the means by which the body grows and builds itself up in love, as each part does its work. If substantial change is going to come, it will come through the church, and the *local* church is the focus, as far as the New Testament is concerned. That is where we are called to work and that is where we can all contribute to making a difference. So what priorities ought we to look for as we travel together into the new century?

1. We need more gospel churches
We have to acknowledge, in penitence, that we have lost and are still losing some great gospel churches of the past to what turns out to be another gospel. Throughout the century this has been happening by subtracting from the Biblical message. The old liberalism is still alive and well, though it often lives under new, fashionable titles, such as 'open evangelicalism'. Although a certain Biblical vocabulary is often in place, all the doors are left open and invaders with an unbiblical agenda tend to make themselves at home. On the other hand, we are still seeing gospel churches are lost by addition to the Biblical message in terms of a new, contemporary spirituality, which is usually attractive because it appears to be deeper or more authentic. In either case, it is no longer enough to talk about Bible-based ministry. Sadly, it is all too possible to use the Bible as a base but not to allow its inerrancy or sufficiency to be the controlling factor in our preaching or practice. We need thoroughly Biblical ministries, in which not only content, but methodology, are

equally submitted to Scripture. The ways in which our churches are led and developed are not theologically neutral. They must come out of the gospel, not simply being built on the pragmatism of what seems to have been successful elsewhere. One of our greatest needs then will be to reclaim churches for the gospel and to plant new churches in which the gospel really is the top of the agenda.

Undoubtedly, one of the major areas of encouragement is the opportunity for evangelical ministry to be received, and welcomed, in churches in which the gospel priority has been lost over the years. It is encouraging to see that many churches, knowing that they need fresh life, rather than close their doors will open the possibility of a new gospel ministry. Situations like this in which change has to be carefully managed and resulting conflicts dealt with in a thoroughly Christian way, are not an easy option. We shall need to work hard together to see what strategies are working, and to provide support networks for those who are venturing out into uncharted waters. But it must be right to try to seize such opportunities if we possibly can.

However, at the same time, we need to be planting new churches. We find that hard to do, because it is a high-risk strategy. Part of our ethos is an inherent conservatism which does not want to try anything, until we are sure it will succeed! But if the experience of the last decade has anything to teach us, it is that in this area we shall learn greatly from our mistakes, and we need to give one another permission to get things wrong, in order to learn how to do things right, in terms of the 21st century. Perhaps we sometimes forget that the big picture of the whole Bible is the gospel. If that ceases to be the dynamic that energises us, it will soon cease to be the heartbeat and distinguishing factor of our ministries and churches. For example, it is possible that our concern for systematics allows our ministries to be diverted from the Biblical 'big picture', which is the gospel itself, into the minutiae of particular doctrines. Sadly, evangelical churches have often become characterised by a constantly narrowing concept of orthodoxy, rather than being thrilled and set on fire with the riches and depth of the gospel. But if we take the whole sweep of Biblical theology seriously, we shall want to define ourselves, first and foremost, as gospel people.

The corollary of that is, however, important to notice. It means we will *not* define ourselves as denominationalists. Of course, we may belong to a particular denomination out of conviction and with real commitment, but it is vital that we do not make an idol of it, whatever its pedigree and strengths may seem to us to be. The new century will need churches where the gospel matters more than the way we have done things in the past or are doing them now. As Biblical evangelicals, we need to commit ourselves to the goal of the evangelisation of our nation, in practical priorities, as well as pious theory. Would it not be a wonderful advance, if in every population centre, in the coming century, there was a living gospel church, bearing an active and credible witness to the Truth, so that any young person wanting to find out about Christianity would be able to hear that message credibly proclaimed and explained, and see it being lived out, in love, irrespective of whatever label such a church might wear? Surely, we must pray and work for gospel churches, across the denominational barriers. We can recognise and respect the different historical streams from which we have come, so long as they do not matter as much as the gospel does. That will challenge us into thinking through new sorts of initiatives. For example, is it really necessary for Baptists and paedo-Baptists to have to plant distinctively different congregations, with half the effect and twice the effort, when they might agree for the sake of the gospel, to work together? Is there not a danger that our views of baptism, however important they may be to us, ultimately are seen to matter more than the gospel itself? These are the issues that we need to be exploring within the fellowship generated by this Assembly and the ongoing work of the Proclamation

Trust. Our literature speaks of 'a fellowship of like-minded evangelicals across denominational lines for encouragement in this exacting work'. That fellowship is a growing reality, as this conference indicates, and we need to work together, to develop the trust and mutual confidence on which new gospel initiatives can be based.

Such networking urgently needs to happen at a local level, with existing churches, where this necessary expansion can begin. It has been observed, I think with some accuracy, that the church growth movement of the 1980s and early 1990s was often concerned about the growth of *my* church, without reference to *yours*, or perhaps even in direct competition. There was sometimes an element of empire-building, which led to a wrong definition of successful ministry, in terms of power, size and status. But such priorities seem very contrary to the words of the Lord Jesus, 'I will build my church.' Yet nothing threatens the status quo and challenges our failures as clearly as planting new congregations. However, it remains true that today's young people will not be won through church structures which are simply the entrenchment of a traditional evangelical methodology, based in the 1950s or 1960s. Manifestly, that is not happening. So, we must think radically about what 'church' means Biblically and be prepared to sit loose to other considerations. We need new vision, expressed in experiments like The Crowded House in Sheffield and the Church on the Corner in Islington. We need wealthier churches not simply to go on adding to their own staff, but to support strategic workers in areas where finances are thin. We need to identify and equip gifted young people, whose ministry might well be in pioneering new works. We need people with energy and vision to think creatively about how to reach the numerous unreached people groups within the UK, let alone further afield. Above all, we need to be in touch with each other about how this can be done. So, as we go back to our own churches and local areas, it would be good to initiate discussion and prayer together with like-minded people on how these issues impact our part of God's world. We need more gospel churches.

2. We need more Biblically-literate Christians

That is to say, they need to be more literate and we need more of them! So, this priority challenges us to ask what we are doing to teach and train others. There is little doubt that we are weaker than we need be in church life generally, because there is such an elementary level of knowledge of the Bible and even less of Biblical theology among us as Christian people. Even when congregations know what they believe and why, we remain comparatively weak in articulating our faith, in the context of today's issues. So often Christians are on the defensive, or simply silent. But if we really believe the Bible's emphasis on the fact that every Christian is given the responsibility of being a minister, or servant, then at the very least, *we* have the equivalent responsibility of seeking to train and equip our fellow believers, to the very best of our ability. In such a context, it is remarkable to think how little input we actually have. In many churches, the only teaching that is done is through the Sunday morning sermon, which may be 20 or 30 minutes at the most. Increasingly, even committed Christians are attending church only once on a Sunday, so that our teaching opportunities are distinctly limited. For the keener members who can make it, there may be a small group programme, perhaps weekly or less frequently, and with a variable educational or teaching input. Often, such groups become more of a fellowship and support network, together with prayer, which is valuable in itself, but is not really helping to equip God's people for works of service. Even on Sundays, it is increasingly uncommon for the majority of the congregation to be present on a weekly basis. Indeed, regular church attendance can mean fortnightly, or even monthly, in some situations. Add to that the problem of potential key leaders having to work very long hours and arriving at home either too late or too exhausted to join in mid-week meetings, and you have a recipe for a malnourished, anaemic, weakened congregation. The churches of the 21st century will need to re-examine our current patterns of nurture and education, and ask just how effective they really are.

Of course, situations like this have faced us in previous generations. In his book, *Evangelicalism in Britain 1935-95*, Oliver Barclay examines the recovery of Biblical evangelicalism, which he calls 'classic evangelicalism', in the post-war period and lists a number of causative factors.[1] Striking among the characteristics of those who recovered evangelical faith at that time, are the facts that they loved Biblical doctrine, embraced a Biblical world-view, and wanted to love God with their minds. Their love of doctrine gave that generation discernment and strength in depth, whereas comparatively few of us in the present generation have been given really unshakeable theological foundations in our training. The sad separation of the Old Testament from the New has mitigated against any coherent Biblical theology, to give us an overview of the message of the whole book, and many of our churches are ignorant of the central message of the whole Bible. Their Biblical world-view, centred on the lordship of Christ, enabled them to enter into a fruitful dialogue with the thought-life of their culture and to apply the Bible's diagnosis and remedies to a wide variety of intellectual, social and personal issues. That was why they wanted to love God with their minds. Their God was big enough to dwarf their human intellects, although many of them were extremely able people, in human terms. They were content to submit in awe to the divine revelation. These are particularly telling points at our stage in the story, since some of us, as their heirs, have emphasised redemption to the exclusion of creation. The danger is always that we shut ourselves into a withdrawn pietism, which can easily become a ghetto, from which we emerge only on hit-and-run evangelistic raids. Such a pattern makes us content with a superficial Biblical understanding, operating only within traditional vocabulary and thought-structures, so that we are effectively cut off from the issues and debates of contemporary culture. The tragedy is that when that is happening, unwittingly or not, we foster an anti-intellectualism which ultimately loses the next generation. It is important to encourage a Biblical world-view among our young people and to stimulate them to learn to love God with their minds.

There is a need for us to examine our teaching programmes, closely and critically, at every level of church life. For example, what is the Sunday School material we are using actually conveying to our children? Does it fall into legalism and moralising? Is it really gospel-centred? Does it teach grace, or does it foster an incipient works religion? The same is true of teenagers' work. If we simply focus on topics, issues and problems in an inductive way, we may generate a pooling of opinions, but that can often degenerate into a sharing of ignorance. However, the alternative must not be a few carefully chosen proof texts, or pat answers. We need to be teaching our young people to think Biblically and encouraging them to apply their understanding to the contemporary issues they are facing, so that they learn to act responsibly on the basis of their own thought-out Biblical convictions. In turn, that will involve training and equipping our teachers, using all the means at our disposal. At the very least, we must seek to encourage good Bible-handling skills and a sound understanding of Biblical theology for anyone who is going to have a leading or teaching role in the congregation. These small groups in a church must not become a breeding ground for un-Biblical ideas. We cannot adopt a *laissez-faire* policy and allow anyone who has time and willingness to assume a 'ministry'. Rather, we need to identify those with the requisite gifts and commitment and concentrate upon equipping them really well. We can be thankful that there are many good training resources available and an increasing network of experience in these areas. We have a huge education job ahead of us, and we all need both to be teaching and learning, on an ongoing basis.

3. We need more varied structures of ministry
Inevitably, the shape of local church ministry is changing and will continue to change. Although some denominational structures may try to hold things together by increasing centralisation, already the impetus is not from the top down, but from the local churches outwards. We therefore need to think creatively about building ministry-teams, which actually set about getting the job done. The development of practical Biblical skills, in good handling of Scripture, coupled with ministry training and experience through 'on the job'-apprenticeships will undoubtedly develop in the coming years. We shall therefore need to develop a flexibility in our training goals and methods, in order to meet the different demands of our changing cultural context.

For example, at present, youth work is a huge area of need in our churches. Many ministers know how difficult it is to try to find staff who have both the Biblical skills and the relational abilities to deal with young people effectively. It seems especially difficult to find those who can teach the young people the Bible in an accurate and compelling way. Not everyone will want to be a long-term youth worker, with professional qualifications, but short-term and part-time roles are other ways of meeting what are huge and growing needs. Work in schools is another area of immense opportunity, where local churches are beginning to combine resources in order to support one or more full-time workers, to take assemblies and Religious Studies lessons and after-school clubs.

Women's work is another area of both need and opportunity. Irrespective of views about women's ordination, church ministry teams are enormously strengthened by the input of well-trained women workers. Pastoral work among women, one-to-one evangelism and nurturing, encouraging and teaching women in their roles both in employment and in the family, as well as a wide-ranging input to the care ministries of the church, these are just a few of the areas crying out for help and attention. All these vital ministries need good handling of Scripture and practical ministry training and experience, and it is often possible for this to start in a part-time capacity and to develop as the ministry does, along with the needed support.

It is especially important to identify, affirm and foster the gifts of our young people. We need to be training and equipping them now for the real world of the coming century. That will certainly demand pioneer evangelists, church planters and builders. We need to recapture our old emphasis on work among children and young people. One of the least developed resources is that of young professionals, many of whom have been converted while students, and who often find the transition from university to work daunting enough, let alone in a church context, where they fit into neither the youth group nor the young marrieds. There is such a wastage of twenty-somethings from active service, often because there is no focus on, or appropriate training for, them. They do not give up being Christian, but they often pour all their energy into their jobs and begin to develop a lifestyle in which church involvement, gospel work and Christian service can play a decreasing role. They easily drift into a consumerist attitude to church: you go for what you can get out of it. Faith becomes a privatised reality, and once-keen gospel people gradually merge into the secular culture. Of course, we want to encourage them to live in the real world and not to dominate their lives with a totally church-oriented agenda, but we cannot afford that sort of wastage.

4. We need more sacrificial servants
I do not imagine that being a Christian in the 21st century is going to get easier! So, we shall need a realism in our

evangelism which counts the cost, and an emphasis in our discipleship on taking up the cross to follow Christ. If we are going to be faithful messengers of a crucified Saviour, we must not be surprised when we are criticised and rejected as he was. Above all, we shall need to model his sacrificial love as he gave himself up for others. We follow a Christ who went through the suffering to glory. But our problem is that we are easily weakened in our resolves by our desire for comfort and an easy life. In world terms, most of us who are full-time Christian workers in the West are well paid, well fed and well housed. There is nothing wrong with that and we should be truly thankful to God for his blessings. A few churches still fail in their duty to support their pastors adequately, but for most of us that is not the issue. Indeed, in some churches, money is the least of the problems. Church members are more than willing to give generously, if it pays for others to do the serving they would rather not have to undertake. But if it is true that 'the only thing that counts is faith expressing itself through love' (Gal. 5:6), then it will be increasingly vital for the church of the 21st century to model that sort of sacrificial love. Indeed, a love that gives itself to others in an increasingly dysfunctional and disconnected society may prove to be the strongest demonstration of the reality of the gospel we preach. As soon as anything else displaces the crucified Christ at the centre of the church's life and message, service will disappear out of the door. So there is no room for careerism in the ministry.

To be a loving church that welcomes people who are starved of relationships that satisfy, and to provide an environment of real Christian friendship and support, is an enormously challenging task. When Paul told the Thessalonians that he was delighted to have shared 'not only the gospel, but our own selves...because you had become so dear to us' (1 Thess. 2:8), we must not forget that that meant 'working night and day...not to be a burden to them'

(2:9). It involved sacrifice, which reminds us of the words of the Lord Jesus that those who have 'much love' for God and for others are those who know that they have been 'much forgiven'. So let us not lose our focus on Christ and living for him. We need to set the standards high in terms of our dedication to the Lord's service. Not a few Christians are keen to be leaders today, but before we can effectively lead we need to be taught to serve. Of course, we are not to be workaholics, ignoring our families or ruining our health. This lifestyle is not a matter of programming, rather it issues from a heart attitude, which goes out of our way to love others, to care for them and to give ourselves in prayer and costly service for their salvation and upbuilding. As has been wisely said, 'The contemporary church does not need more salesmen of the gospel, but more free samples.'

5. We need more spiritual realism

I sometimes fear that we are our own worst enemies, because we refuse to come to the end of our human resources. Much of what I have been saying could be construed in that way, as simply demanding more effort, energy and investment from the human point of view. But, without the breath of God's Spirit and the intervention of God's grace, nothing of lasting value will happen. It must be one of the greatest tragedies of the last thirty years to see the polarisation of thinking about the Word and the Spirit in evangelical church life. In reacting rightly against a me-centred, experience-dominated spirituality, we have sometimes conducted our ministries as though they were self sufficient and independent of God's gracious enabling. If we are going to face the demands of our culture now and in the future, we must return to a right view of these two indispensable ingredients of gospel ministry. It is still the gracious work of the Spirit of God to take the Word of God in order to produce the people of God. Or, as J. I. Packer puts it,

God's Spirit teaches us through Scripture. The Spirit of Christ
who indwells Christians never leads them to doubt, criticize,
go beyond, or fall short of Bible teaching. Spirits which do that
are not the Spirit of Christ (1 John 4:1-6). Rather, the Holy
Spirit makes us appreciate the divine authority of Scripture, so
that we accept its account of spiritual realities and live as it
calls us to do. As the Spirit gave the Word by brooding over its
human writers and leading the church to recognize their books
as its canon for belief and behaviour, so now he becomes the
authoritative interpreter of Scripture as he shows us how biblical
teaching bears on our living. To be sure, what Bible books
meant as messages to their first readers can be gleaned from
commentaries. But what they mean for our lives today is
something we learn only as the Spirit stirs our insensitive
consciences. Never does the Spirit draw us away from the
written Word, any more than from the living Word. Instead, he
keeps us in constant, conscious, contented submission to both
together.[2]

Until that sort of realism grips our minds and hearts, we
will not really be praying people; and until we become praying
people again, we shall always be enfeebled and impoverished
people. Not only do we need healthy Biblical realism about
fantasy Christianity, with its dreams and delusions, we also
need healthy Biblical realism about our own sluggishness,
our compromise, our intellectual arrogance, our self-reliance
and independence from God. If we are to see the gospel
proclaimed in power and the Lord Jesus honoured,
worshipped and adored in our land, the church of the 21st
century will be a church on her knees at the cross, united
with Christ in his death, that we may be raised up with him
in his power. She will be a church of repentance and total
dependence on the God of grace, a church which knows that
the way into the Christian life is also the way on in the
Christian life; a church which is humble under God's mighty
hand, so that in due time (his and not hers) he may lift her up.
And when God lifts his people up, he sends us into his world,

with his Word in our hands, on our lips and in our hearts, to proclaim its Truth, in love, knowing that this is God's work from start to finish, and that anything which will stand the test of his judgment fire is accomplished by his power alone and exists solely for his glory. It will be a church that is governed and dominated by a passionate commitment to the end of the story; a church that lives in time, but for eternity.

> I did not see a temple in the city, because the Lord God Almighty and the Lamb are its temple. The city does not need the sun or the moon to shine on it, for the glory of God gives it light, and the Lamb is its lamp. The nations will walk by its light, and the kings of the earth will bring their splendour into it. On no day will its gates ever be shut, for there will be no night there. The glory and honour of the nations will be brought into it. Nothing impure will ever enter it, nor will anyone who does what is shameful or deceitful, but only those whose names are written in the Lamb's book of life (Rev. 21:22-27).

Notes
1. Oliver Barclay, *Evangelicalism in Britain 1935-95*, IVP, 1997.
2. J.I. Packer, *Truth and Power*, Eagle, p. 39.

13

'AM I ONLY A GOD NEARBY AND NOT A GOD FAR AWAY'
(Jeremiah 23:23)

David Jackman

'AM I ONLY A GOD NEARBY AND NOT A GOD FAR AWAY'
(Jeremiah 23:23)

David Jackman

As we come to the close of this year's Assembly, let me remind you of the title that has over-arched all our sessions – 'Doing God's work God's way.' It might well be seen as a typical 'Proc. Trust' title, don't you think? Typical of the arrogance of conservative evangelicals who think they are the sole custodians of divine truth and the exclusive practitioners of God's will. But typical not only of their narrow-mindedness, but of their small-mindedness as well! The two run together, of course. Only the very naïve could imagine that in a culture as complex as ours, and as varied in its beliefs and practices, in the global village of the 21st century, it could ever again be feasible to talk about right and wrong, good or evil. Who could ever know what God's work would look like? Or, who would presume to think his way is not seen in the multiplicity of religious options and the burgeoning pluralism which is so strongly marketed as our only hope for the future? What sort of a world do these Proclamation Trust people live in?

Most of you know the arguments as well as I do and can probably rehearse them more penetratingly. By a few deft touches, 2,000 years of Biblical theology is swept away in the flood of cultural relativism. Perhaps the greatest danger today is that many an evangelical institution, local congregation, not to mention thousands of individual Christians, will be caught up in that vortex. For it is a flood tide, and not to 'go with the flow' is to relegate oneself to

what appears to be an unimportant backwater. That is the
reality of the world to which we return from the Assembly.
We shall meet it not only in the media, but in the synods and
councils of our denominations, in some of the training courses
provided for ministry, and even in the committees of our
local congregations. The battle is still on for Truth, as it has
been in every generation, but the weapons of the Internet and
the carefully edited 'sound-bite' may prove much more
invasive and difficult to counteract than the infidel's sword.
However, because 'there is nothing new under the sun', I
want to turn you to Jeremiah 23, for some encouragement
and focus, and to take up verse 23 as the theme verse. I think
we shall see it's the key to opening up this whole section
from verses 9-40, about the false prophets.

> [9]Concerning the prophets:
> My heart is broken within me;
>   all my bones tremble.
> I am like a drunken man,
>   like a man overcome by wine,
> because of the LORD
>   and his holy words.
> [10]The land is full of adulterers;
>   because of the curse the land lies parched
>   and the pastures in the desert are withered.
> The prophets follow an evil course
>   and use their power unjustly.
> [11]'Both prophet and priest are godless;
>   even in my temple I find their wickedness,'
>   declares the LORD.
> [12]'Therefore their path will become slippery;
>   they will be banished to darkness
>   and there they will fall.
> I will bring disaster on them
>   in the year they are punished,'
>   declares the LORD.
> [13]'Among the prophets of Samaria
>   I saw this repulsive thing:

They prophesied by Baal
    and led my people Israel astray.
¹⁴And among the prophets of Jerusalem
    I have seen something horrible:
    They commit adultery and live a lie.
They strengthen the hands of evildoers,
    so that no-one turns from his wickedness.
They are all like Sodom to me;
    the people of Jerusalem are like Gomorrah.'

¹⁵Therefore, this is what the LORD Almighty says concerning
the prophets:

'I will make them eat bitter food
    and drink poisoned water,
because from the prophets of Jerusalem
    ungodliness has spread throughout the land.'

¹⁶This is what the LORD Almighty says:

'Do not listen to what the prophets are prophesying to you;
    they fill you with false hopes.
They speak visions from their own minds,
    not from the mouth of the LORD.
¹⁷They keep saying to those who despise me,
    "The LORD says: You will have peace."
And to all who follow the stubbornness of their hearts
    they say, "No harm will come to you."
¹⁸But which of them has stood in the council of the LORD
    to see or to hear his word?
    Who has listened and heard his word?
¹⁹See, the storm of the LORD
    will burst out in wrath,
a whirlwind swirling down
    on the heads of the wicked.
²⁰The anger of the LORD will not turn back
    until he fully accomplishes
    the purposes of his heart.
In days to come
    you will understand it clearly.

²¹I did not send these prophets,
    yet they have run with their message;
I did not speak to them,
    yet they have prophesied.
²²But if they had stood in my council,
    they would have proclaimed my words to my people
and would have turned them from their evil ways
    and from their evil deeds."

²³'Am I only a God nearby,'

                                        declares the LORD,

    'and not a God far away?
²⁴Can anyone hide in secret places
    so that I cannot see him?'

                                        declares the LORD.

    'Do not I fill heaven and earth?'

                                        declares the LORD.

²⁵'I have heard what the prophets say who prophesy lies in my name. They say, "I had a dream! I had a dream!" ²⁶How long will this continue in the hearts of these lying prophets, who prophesy the delusions of their own minds? ²⁷They think the dreams they tell one another will make my people forget my name, just as their fathers forgot my name through Baal worship. ²⁸Let the prophet who has a dream tell his dream, but let the one who has my word speak it faithfully. For what has straw to do with grain?' declares the LORD. ²⁹Is not my word like fire,' declares the LORD, 'and like a hammer that breaks a rock in pieces?

³⁰'Therefore,' declares the LORD, 'I am against the prophets who steal from one another words supposedly from me. ³¹Yes,' declares the LORD, 'I am against the prophets who wag their own tongues and yet declare, "The LORD declares." ³²Indeed, I am against those who prophesy false dreams,' declares the LORD. 'They tell them and lead my people astray with their reckless lies, yet I did not send or appoint them. They do not benefit these people in the least,' declares the LORD.

³³'When these people, or a prophet or a priest, ask you, "What is the oracle of the LORD?" say to them, "What oracle?

I will forsake you, declares the LORD." ³⁴If a prophet or a priest or anyone else claims, "This is the oracle of the LORD," I will punish that man and his household. ³⁵This is what each of you keeps on saying to his friend or relative: "What is the LORD's answer?" or "What has the LORD spoken?" ³⁶But you must not mention "the oracle of the LORD" again, because every man's own word becomes his oracle and so you distort the words of the living God, the LORD Almighty, our God. ³⁷This is what you keep saying to a prophet: "What is the LORD's answer to you?" or "What has the LORD spoken?" ³⁸Although you claim, "This is the oracle of the LORD," this is what the LORD says: You used the words, "This is the oracle of the LORD," even though I told you that you must not claim, "This is the oracle of the LORD." ³⁹Therefore, I will surely forget you and cast you out of my presence along with the city I gave to you and your fathers. ⁴⁰I will bring upon you everlasting disgrace – everlasting shame that will not be forgotten.'

Jeremiah is prophesying at *the* crucial moment in the titanic battle for truth which has been raging in Judah. The first twenty chapters of the book are a devastating inventory of Judah's sin and rebellion, which are about to lead to the fall of the southern kingdom and the exile of its people. At chapter 21, we move into a new mode which we might define as analysis. The chapter is a review of the kings of David's house. First the present king, Zedekiah, whose name ironically means 'the LORD is my righteousness', is dealt with (21:7). Then a judgment against the whole house of David is issued in 21:12-14. After setting out the principles of what kingship should be, there is a series of judgments levelled at different kings in chapter 22 – Shallum or Jehoahaz (vv. 11-12), Jehoiakim (vv. 18-19) and Jehoiachin (vv. 25-27). Verse 30 is a solemn conclusion, declaring what seems to be the end of the Davidic line: 'For none of his offspring will prosper, none will sit on the throne of David or rule any more in Judah.'

So, we come into chapter 23 asking the question, 'Has

God totally repudiated the Covenant he made with David?'
The chapter starts by denouncing the shepherds (leaders, king
and his ministers). 'Shepherd' is, of course, a Biblical image
of kingship (as when David acknowledged the LORD as his
shepherd in Psalm 23:1). But it continues with a promise
that *the* Shepherd, the LORD himself, will intervene personally.
There are promises of restoration and prosperity (Jer. 23:3),
and of new and properly functioning shepherds (v. 4). Indeed,
verses 5-6 point to a new era, unspecified in time, when
from Jesse's stump a new shoot, a righteous Branch, will
appear, and his name will reveal his nature. Unlike Zedekiah
('my righteousness is the LORD') this king will be 'the LORD
our Righteousness', in the fulfilment of all the Davidic
promises. He will prove to be the divine ruler, who is utterly
righteous; a perfect shepherd-king.

But at verse 9 the focus swings back to the present situation
of desperate need, in Jeremiah's Jerusalem, with a devastating
analysis of why things are as they are 'concerning the
prophets'. It is an important Old Testament insight to
recognise that prophecy began to develop in 1 Samuel,
parallel with the monarchy. The reason is clear. It was God's
revelation, through the prophets, which would keep the king
within the government and control of the LORD. The prophets
came as 'Covenant Law Enforcement Mediators'. This is
the memorable title and role highlighted by Gordon Fee and
Douglas Stewart, in their treatment of the prophets, in *How
To Read the Bible for All Its Worth*. Their role was critical.
If there is a word from the LORD then it will be both infallible
in its content and sufficient in its scope. Deuteronomy 29:29:
'The secret things belong to the LORD our God, but the things
revealed belong to us and to our children forever, that we
may follow all the words of this law.' Therefore, the greatest
of all dangers to the people of God will be lying prophets,
or in New Testament terms, 'false teachers'. They have all
the outward appearances of authentication and approval, but
no authorisation from God. They were not doing his work,

let alone doing it his way, and yet the tide was running with them.

This was the immense challenge that Jeremiah faced personally, as he endeavoured to proclaim God's truth, the whole truth, and nothing but the truth to his unbelieving countrymen. Jerusalem is about to fall as God's righteous judgment against their sin and rebellion is finally let loose, but he is the only voice proclaiming that message, and all the other 'prophets' flatly contradict him. They were the mainstream, on the cutting edge of contemporary relevance, and alongside them Jeremiah was about as relevant as a cultural dinosaur. It isn't hard to see that the problem of 6th century Judah is exactly the problem of the late 20th century. What is the LORD's Word, for today? Where does the authority lie? For example, are contemporary church leaders right when they declare that the law of Moses is no longer binding on Christians, so that we can ignore the description in Leviticus 18:22 of homosexual activity as 'detestable' to the Lord? Is the view correct that Paul's classification of homosexual practice as sin shows that 'he did not understand human nature'? Or are they false prophets? It's a very live issue, isn't it? Or what about the declaration of a whole group of prophets in the USA that the last days began in 1990 and there are only forty years left during which an elite group of believers will perform signs and wonders, stretch out their hands to immobilise Christ's enemies and gain extraordinary supernatural power in the nations, to prepare the way for Christ's return? True or false? Your answer will have a huge effect on how you live and what sort of priorities you develop within your ministry and your congregation.

So we are dealing with the most relevant, live issues when we come to Jeremiah 23 for help, aren't we? Why do I suggest that verse 23 is the key? Because the domestication of God has led to the seduction of the pulpit. Clearly the LORD's question in this verse challenges the presuppositions of the false prophets. 'Am I only a God nearby,' declares the LORD, 'and not a God far away?' Here is the root of their error. Because they have domesticated God and made him pocket-sized, they have begun to imagine that he can be manipulated. They have lost any real concept of the awesomeness of God. He is simply one piece, among others, on the chessboard of religious theory; a factor in their equations – an ingredient in their religious discussions, but not the God of verse 24. 'Can anyone hide in secret places so that I cannot see him?' declares the LORD. 'Do not I fill heaven and earth?' He is not the God of shattering omniscience, not the God of universal omnipresence, not the God of sovereign omnipotence – *not* the LORD! Some may have imagined him to be like any other tribal deity, active and effective only within certain restricted geographical parameters. Others seem to have thought he was only around when *they* chose to think about him. His existence and his properties required *their* permission for them to function. Either way, God was thoroughly domesticated. He was at the end of their rope, under their patronage, and as a result, totally devoid of their respect. That is why they claimed to speak for him. You cannot be a false prophet if you have any true reverence for Yahweh. They had remade him in their own imagination and in their own image, and so divine reve-lation was replaced by 'the assured fruits of contemporary scholarship' and the message that people want to hear. Now once that has happened, the pulpit will be totally seduced by the culture! All you have to listen to are the words of men. They may appear superficially attractive and promise all sorts of comfort and joy, but ultimately, they are just the words of men – transient and powerless.

We don't find it too hard to see that in the more open and flagrant departures from Biblical truth within many of the denominations. But of course we can easily forget that *we* are never immune to the pressures of the culture we live in. One of the most important aspects of spiritual preventive medicine is to see where we ourselves are being squeezed into the world's mould, and surely it would not be at all surprising if the pulpit/teaching ministry was the focus of contemporary attack by the enemy.

Jeremiah helpfully exposes the hidden causes of the problem in his own day, in a way that can provide a pattern for our own analysis. For as the New Testament apostle warns us, 'There were false prophets among the people just as there will be false teachers among you. They will secretly introduce destructive heresies...' (2 Pet. 2:1). Notice that there is a significant progression through the passage. In verses 11-15, the prophet identifies the lifestyle which is the product and evidence of false prophecy. In verses 16-22, he moves in closer to discover its contents and then lastly in verses 25-32, we see its root cause. The order is important to follow, because the symptoms are the sign of the disease.

1. Godless lifestyle (verses 11-15)

The end of verse 15 points out that ungodliness, alienation from the LORD, is endemic throughout the land, but verse 11 has already identified the cause: 'both prophet and priest are godless.' They are godless themselves and they spread godlessness through their 'ministry'. So what the religious leaders practise and tolerate is not a matter of privacy; it has an impact throughout the nation. The false prophet is known by his own lifestyle and by what his preaching produces in the life-styles of others. Verse 13 expresses it cogently: 'Among the prophets of Samaria I saw this repulsive thing: They prophesied by Baal and led my people Israel astray.' It was comparatively easy to see the reasons for the demise of Israel, the Northern Kingdom, through the apostasy of the Baal worship in which they had indulged. Their preachers had actually used the name of the false god to turn Israel away from loyalty to her Covenant Lord. But although such blatant polytheism was not visible in Jerusalem, yet its inhabitants 'live a lie' (verse 14). Literally, they go after the lie – a name for Baal, or any other false gods. Jerusalem is bereft of a ministry of truth. There is no-one to challenge the sins of the people, from the Word of the living God. The reason is that the preachers are practising those very sins themselves (verse 10a: 'The land is full of adulterers').

The visible world of time and sense has become far more important to them than the unseen God and his eternal Word, so that they were only too ready to give religious approval to what God saw as gross sin. This is the theology of 'I'm OK; you're OK' where nothing can be totally ruled out, especially if it's done in private and not harming others. It ends in the godlessness of Sodom and Gomorrah. This is the religious climate where therapy replaces theology, testimony replaces truth and fantasy replaces Biblical fact. Wherever there is a multiplication of idolatry and immorality in the church you can always be sure that the pulpit has been seduced. The preachers have become children of their age, and even in the temple (the church of the living God), wickedness is found. 'Both prophet and priest are godless; even in my temple I find their wickedness, declares the LORD.' Integrity and godliness of character are the essential undergirding and confirmation of the reality of true ministry and faithful ministers.

2. Delusive content (verses 16-22)
The vision they proclaim is self-induced. It does not originate with God at all. In verse 16b 'false hopes' literally means 'delusions', 'vanities', or 'a bag of wind'. What the preachers proclaim are just words, without any reality at all. Verse 18 is devastatingly explicit. 'But which of them has stood in the council of the LORD to see or to hear his word? Who has listened and heard his word?' Had they been listening to God, they would not have contradicted what he had already said in the Law and the Covenant. But verse 17 shows that this contradiction was the very heart of their 'message'. There was a deliberate refusal to recognise that God must judge evil, and so they promised peace and safety to those who

were heading straight for God's wrath. Because they wanted to live worldly, godless lives, they pretended that God would tolerate what he defines as sin. It is always a mark of false prophets that they pander to the spirit of the age and become the victims of their own imaginations. The pulpit gradually becomes more and more worldly. The rest of the section makes it clear that it is the demand for repentance and the certainty of God's wrath that have been evacuated from their sermons. But we need to search our own hearts and honestly to ask whether we are being seduced by the spirit of our age, the values of our culture.

How much 'meat of the Word' is there in our preaching? Many evangelical pulpits devote more time and energy to clever contemporarising (the latest film, TV or pop culture ideas), using witty parallels of Biblical truth, verbal cartoons, funny stories, sound-bite attractiveness, rather than serious unpacking of Biblical truth. Sit on a committee choosing speakers for an evangelical event, and as names are considered, listen to the criteria used to evaluate them. 'Too heavy, too serious, not enough humour, too cerebral.' Please don't misunderstand me! I am emphatically not pleading for long, boring, dry sermons, but are we being seduced by the culture? We can tell if we are, because like the false prophets of Jeremiah's day, and those in New Testament times, we shall be using the wrong criteria in evaluating our preaching. What makes for good preaching today? Intellectual respectability is one value. This accounts for our exaggerated deference to academic criticism, imbibed from college days onwards, which gives just enough unresolved doubts about God's Word to prevent it being preached with conviction and power. Audience approval is another. This explains why we are so competitive, in case someone else steals the sheep by a more attractive show down the road. Cultural acceptability predominates, which means that affirmation is more important than confrontation or challenge and that the message must be tuned to the current

cultural norms, rather than the culture being confronted by
the Truth. It is the spiritual equivalent of political correctness.
So there is no edge to the preaching, no getting under the
skin. It becomes the rehearsal of the familiar, increasingly
bland ideas, the well-worn phrases and clichés, inducing
complacency. Where there is no penetrating critique, the
culture remains king. The people of God are not strengthened,
or even fed, and gradually, but relentlessly, the church takes
on the values of the world, in areas of work, gender, marriage,
etc. The pulpit becomes the habitat of the wind-bag, seduced
and nullified. Why?

3. False authority (verses 25-32)
The false prophets' authority base lies within themselves.
On the basis of a dream, they prophesy lies in the Lord's
name (verse 25). Lying dreams are the product of deluded
minds (verse 26). But the root of the problem is that they are
looking within for the ground of truth, rather than submitting
to the divine revelation. There is no 'inner light' that can
provide divine guidance. Rather it is God's Word, from
outside of us, that provides the lamp for our feet and the light
for our path. That is why they are inevitably led to the
delusions of verse 27. False prophecy can have just as
devastating an effect as Baal worship. In fact, the two are
inextricably linked. The false religions all around in
Jeremiah's day considered dreams to be of great significance.
This was how one might discover the will of the gods. When
you have only your own imagination to rely on, a dream
seems to have a bit more of the mystical or spiritual about it
at least. And of course it is wonderfully slippery, leaving
the maximum room for manoeuvre, which is what false
prophecy thrives on. This internal authority explains verse
30 as well. 'Therefore,' declares the LORD, 'I am against the
prophets who steal from one another words supposedly from
me.' They steal from one another, because they depend on
one another. They need one another's endorsements; they

support one another's paperbacks with their new emphases, and the exciting videos that seem to confirm the truth of what is being taught. You know how it spreads! 'Mr X has said it, so it must be true.' But as the last verses of the chapter make clear, those who distort God's Word and elevate their own ideas in its place, in such a cavalier fashion, face an eternal future of shame and disgrace.

That is where the seduction of the pulpit leads. Every time a preacher says, 'I rather like to think....' or 'In these days we really cannot be tied by the old, traditional view....' and then substitutes his own human arrogance for the Word of the living God, it is exactly the same issue, and God's penetrating question is still vital: 'Am I only a God nearby, and not a God far away?' In how many evangelical conferences today is the Word of God read and then closed, or never even opened? Instead of our minds being directed by our hearts being humbled, our ears are tickled and our sense of humour indulged by a succession of stories and jokes and illustrations which depend on the charisma of the preacher, but all too often evict the Word of God. Do we really believe that the Word will do the work, or are we more concerned about our reputation as preachers. The one is the service of God, the other the service of men.

Verses 28-29 sum it all up, so powerfully. ' "Let the prophet who has a dream tell his dream, but let the one who has my word speak it faithfully. For what has straw to do with grain?" declares the LORD. "Is not my word like fire," declares the LORD, "and like a hammer that breaks a rock in pieces?" ' What is the remedy? It is very simple and very basic. Let the one who has the Word of God speak it faithfully. The rest is chaff; blown away, burned up. The Word is wheat, the bread of life for the people of God. Do not give up on your preaching! Its effect is like fire, burning up the dross and all the rubbish of wrong thinking and wrong living. God's Word is like a hammer, shattering the rock, breaking up what looks so solid, so resistant to God, so immovable. But that

will only happen when the preachers stand in the council of
the Lord. When we listen to his Word alone, then the
experience of Jeremiah in verse 9 will become ours. We
shall know a true brokenness of heart and a real trembling
before God, as we consider who the Lord is, and how he has
revealed himself in his 'holy words'. I believe it to be the
greatest need in the church and in the world that we ministers
should speak that Word faithfully. It is what we pray will be
restored in hundreds of pulpits all across our land. Only that
will turn our nation round, and only that will ensure that we
do the real work of the living God in his way.

'Am I only a God nearby, and not a God far away?'
'For what has straw to do with grain?' declares the LORD.

SCRIPTURE INDEX

SUBJECT INDEX